# Do You Feel Miss . . . Fit With Yourself . . . Others . . . God?

by

Sue Holsinger

ISBN: 978-1-60920-093-0
Printed in the United States of America
©2014 Sue Holsinger
All rights reserved

API
Ajoyin Publishing, Inc.
P.O. 342
Three Rivers, MI 49093
www.ajoyin.com

Please direct your inquiries to admin@ajoyin.com

# Contents

# PREFACE

In this book I share my life and experiences. I am not trained in psychology, nor am I a professional counselor, and none of my suggestions are from that viewpoint. I eagerly share spiritual principles that have been effective in my life and in many others'. Because my heart's passion is to help people unload their painful, emotional baggage, I am pleased to allow you to enter my world from more than twenty years of ministry experience.

. . .

For ease of writing, I'm using the pronoun "he" for many of the examples, but most are not gender specific.

. . .

Scripture references are from the New International Version of the Bible unless otherwise noted.

# MY GRATITUDE

First of all, I want to thank God for Dennis and Susan Brown. I am so grateful to them for introducing me to the baptism of the Holy Spirit. The Holy Spirit, through them, transformed my life. They raised me up in ministry, and the ten years I spent under their spiritual leadership set me on the path for today. For that I will be forever grateful.

. . .

I gave this manuscript to two friends to proofread. I value the opinion of my spiritual mentor and closest friend, who has permission to speak into my life and give me godly counsel. I wanted her to examine the truth of my words. I have never had anyone in my life who has "bright eyes" for me like she does. No matter what is going on, she embraces me with open arms and a warm, loving welcome. Paula Howard Lancaster is not only my pastor; she is a friend that "sticketh closer than a brother." When my husband was diagnosed with advanced lung cancer, she told me, "If this doesn't go how we hope it will and pray that it does, you will not have to walk this alone." The day I called her and said, "This is the last day that I can take Ken out," she arrived at our house with her packed bags and said, "I am here until it's over." I can't tell you what a relief and blessing that was to me and my family.

Paula has experienced many of the issues I present in this book. And through it all, she has embraced the truth of the Word and the healing of Jesus. I am so thankful that I can call her my friend, and am grateful to God, who caused our paths to be joined together. Thank you, Paula, for your friendship and spiritual leadership. You help make the kingdom of God look good.

. . .

My other proofreader is a dear friend who has ministered the light, life, and healing of Jesus to me many times. She was my "go-to" person when I needed help to uncover deep and painful roots that were producing a bountiful harvest of less than godly fruit in my life. I wanted her "knowing eye" to examine this text. Christine Routh is proof that you don't need an official title to be used powerfully by the Lord. She is definitely a huge asset to the kingdom of God, and I am grateful that God gave me a divine connection to Him through Chris.

Chris has authored the book *Boundary Recommendations,* in which she speaks with much experience as she shares her knowledge from ministering to survivors of satanic ritual abuse and gives practical guidelines and boundaries for those who minister to individuals.

Chris and her husband Tom graciously offered me the use of their retreat cabin on several occasions. In fact, it was in their cabin that I began writing this book. That was a wonderful week of solitude, listening to the Lord, and writing. Thank you, Chris, for your friendship and spiritual insight.

. . .

I would like to give a big thank you to my sister-in-law Ina Holsinger for the use of her home while I was in Pennsylvania on vacation. While there, I was able to write another large section of this book in East Sharpsburg, Pennsylvania.

. . .

And to my dear friends Ray and Janet Busfield, I give a huge thank you for the use of their retreat time and condo in northern Michigan. That time was very instrumental in my writing journey. Thank you, friends.

. . .

My greatest praise and gratitude goes to God for all He has done in my life. I am so grateful that Jesus has stepped into my woundedness and brought healing and freedom.

# FORWARD

There are a lot of "self-help" books out there, so why should you pick up this one? The answer is simple; it is written by one who knows firsthand what she is talking about. I have often told our congregation that you can argue theology all day long, but there is no argument for an experience. Sue has firsthand, experiential knowledge of the power that is in practicing the truth of the Word of God.

There is not a person out there that has not had some sort of wounding, disappointment, or unmet expectation. That is just the nature of the beast. Unfortunately, we live in permanent marker, not No. 2 pencil; there is no going back. It becomes a matter of figuring out how to go forward from where we find ourselves right now. This book contains more than testimonies of survival. It is a handbook for being able to move from darkness to light, from sadness to joy, from defeat to victory. *Do You Feel Miss . . . Fit?* offers hope that not every day, every month, every year has to be like this one.

If you are like most of us, you have tried "everything," but it did not give you the results you were counting on. Don't misunderstand; there are many "good ideas" out there, but 1 Corinthians 12:31 refers to the fact that there is "a more excellent way," and that way is the Word of God applied directly to our situations and circumstances. Albert Einstein once said that the significant problems we face cannot be solved at the same level of thinking we were at when they were created. Solutions are available, but they require us to increase our level of understanding and to seek wise counsel from a higher authority, and there is no higher authority than the applied truths of the Word of

God. With the prayers that Sue includes in this book, she gives you one of the most powerful resources known to mankind: that is, God's Word in your mouth.

*Do You Feel Miss . . . Fit?* was written from the perspective of one who went to the well dry and parched and came back refreshed and ready to be used. Mark 14:8 refers to a woman about whom Jesus said, "She did what she could." Sue is just that sort of woman; she is evidence to the fact that there is life after severe wounding and disappointment. It is such good news to realize that problems and failures in no way negate our promise or our potential. I pray for each one who picks up this book and is able to incorporate its strategies. It is my sincere hope that you will be able to come to the realization that God has not changed His mind about you or His plans for you.

I learned long ago that I do not have to make every mistake personally in order to learn from it. Sue has graciously allowed us access to her journey and allowed us the opportunity to learn from her choices, both good and bad; for that, many of us will be forever grateful. She is one of those people who you just know is a better person healed than she would have been had she never been broken, and I am glad to call her my friend.

*Pastor Paula Lancaster*
*Antioch Fellowship Center*

Chapter One

# INTRODUCTION

I believe if all could be told, we would find that feeling like a misfit is far more common than we would have first believed. Many of us may feel out of place in certain settings or situations, but when a person feels like he is a misfit, he feels like he doesn't fit into life. What a desperate way to live. So many people, including Christians, struggle with self-identity issues and feeling as if there is something wrong with them. Christians may even be more troubled about those feelings, because when they got saved, they believed (or at least hoped) that all their past issues would automatically go away. I wish it would happen that way, but I don't believe it does for most people.

I have a dear uncle that had a very transformational experience when he accepted Jesus as his Lord and Savior. Several years before he was introduced to Jesus, he had come to our house to help us winterize our camper. As my husband and I were outside with him learning from his expertise, I had to excuse myself and go inside because I couldn't take all the foul language he was using. Uncle wasn't upset; he was just speaking in his usual manner. Later, when I received the news that Uncle had "gotten saved," I was very eager to go see him. As we sat there and he related how wonderful he was feeling, I was totally amazed at what I was hearing. He told me his desires to smoke and drink were instantly gone. But what astounded me the most was that his language was pure. When I mentioned it to him, he hadn't recognized that change. He didn't even realize how unclean his talk had been. I am still amazed at the magnitude of his transformation. I do believe that that is the ultimate salvation experience, and why we don't all have it happen that way is a mystery to me.

The Word of God tells us in Jeremiah 29:11, *"For I know the plans I have for you . . . plans to prosper you and not to harm you, plans to give you hope and a future."* Believing you don't measure up, aren't good enough, or are unfit in some way greatly diminishes your ability to receive all God has for you; not because He doesn't want to give it to you, but because you would have difficulty believing it or receiving it. When Jesus said He came to give us life to the full, abundant life (John 10:10), I believe He had more in mind than our just "hanging on" or continually struggling with issues of life. By definition, abundant life means superior in quality and quantity. It seems to me that many Christians live far below what God desires for us. If God's plan is for us to have life till it overflows (Amplified Bible) like Jesus said He came to give us, then it has to be possible. As Pastor Paula often says, "If God didn't want me to believe it, He shouldn't have put it in the Book!" If we are not living up to what God desires for us, there have to be reasons.

When a person repents of his sins and asks Jesus to live in his heart, it is difficult to understand how his past sins can all be forgiven and erased but he continues to struggle with many of those old feelings, desires, and habits. It can be frustrating and defeating to know we are supposed to be dead to sin (Romans 6) after we are saved and not be able to live that out. We enter the Christian community believing that Christianity works; so if it works, why is it so hard? Why do I still feel the old way? Why do I want to sin? Why do I still have those old thoughts and desires? Instead of giving you some of the usual religious answers to "read your Bible more, pray harder, or just choose not to think about it," I will give you some understandable spiritual roots and reasons that I believe will be very enlightening to you, and you will have an "ah-ha" moment when you say, "That makes so much sense." And the really good news is that when there are spiritual roots and reasons, there are also spiritual ways to deal with those issues. When I use the term "spiritual roots and reasons," I'm referring to the issues in our hearts—anger, unforgiveness, self-hatred, etc., and things we do that activate an automatic response in the spiritual realm because of sowing and reaping.

Proverbs 13:12 says, *"Hope deferred makes the heart sick."* When a person believes there is no hope for change, he either gives up trying or takes whatever drastic measures seem the best to resolve the situation. A Christian who really tries to rise above his sin or shortcomings and just can't seem to do it often feels shame or guilt, and defeated. I know a young man who believed that he would lose his salvation when he sinned, so every Wednesday and Sunday he would go to the altar to "get right with God" again. He noticed that he was the only one repenting week after week, and he finally came to the conclusion that he wasn't good enough to be saved, God didn't want him, or God wasn't able to save him.

It can be life-crippling to believe, "I am not right." How much more miss-fit could a person feel than when he believes his existence is wrong? No matter what you believe about yourself, if it doesn't line up with the Word of God and who God says you are, there are reasons for your self-beliefs, and hope and healing are available and possible for you.

Many people, especially Christians, are not comfortable telling others how they really feel about themselves. Many times they can't even face it themselves. My pain and self-identity issues were so deeply hidden that it took the Lord's excavation to bring them to the surface. Far too many Christians struggle with, "After all, now that I am a Christian, I should have the mind of Christ, and if I don't, there must be something wrong with me." Sometimes when a person does dare to express his inner struggles with someone, he is told he shouldn't feel that way—as if he didn't already know that! I once witnessed a young woman at a church who was encouraged by a man to express herself honestly. I believe it was the first time she dared to open up and pour out her heart about herself. When she finished, he said, "Okay, you can put your mask back on now." I couldn't believe what I heard him say. How devastating to a vulnerable person.

Christians can get a sense of their value when they embrace the truth of the Word that God loves His children, and they are valuable to Him. They feel some legitimacy when they know they are accepted and loved by God. But I do believe for those who have a serious issue with believing their worth, if their heart of hearts could be exposed, there would still be some self-doubts. It is possible for a Christian to believe he has value because he knows he is loved and accepted by God, but still not feel valued or wanted outside of his Christian life. Even though the advice to read the Bible and pray more, keep telling yourself you are valuable and forgive and forget sound good, I know from personal experience and that of others that the issues under poor self-identity beliefs cannot be changed by just learning more scripture or doing "God things." You could memorize the whole of Scripture and still not have it successfully penetrate the deep wounds in your heart that caused you to accept as true those things you believe about yourself. I fully believe in renewing our minds (Romans 12:2) with Scripture and knowing it so well that it becomes a part of us, but if your heart belief is rooted in pain, it often takes more than quoting a scripture to make it go away.

When you paint over rust with a good paint, it might look more pleasing and seem to have a better sense of wholeness, but the rust is still there, continuing its destruction under the surface. I heard a seminar teaching on "Dead Works" by Dr. Henry Wright, author of *A More Excellent Way,* and he was speaking about rust removal. He said we put on "Jesus paint," but the rust always shows through. I know that no matter how much of God we try to put on, no matter how we try to look good, and no matter how many good works we do, our rust is more powerful than our efforts. Dr. Wright says that God wants to meet you in your rust. Nothing can change rust—it has to be removed. Amen, Dr. Wright.

Even though the distance from your head to your heart is only about twelve inches, it is like a million miles when you try to bridge that gap with head knowledge. The only bridge I have found is Jesus revealing His truth to your heart. Revelation (an eye-opening moment when you get an understanding deep within you that the Word of God is true for you—like the light goes on inside your understanding, and it empowers you to believe it as truth) in your heart or spirit brings the Word to life within you and has a much more profound effect in your life than only knowing it because someone told you or you read it (head knowledge). You have to go to the root or reason under a heart belief to change it. There are reasons rust cannot just be wiped off a surface, and there are spiritual reasons why some wrong self-beliefs cannot be dethroned by just choosing to not believe them anymore or choosing to believe something different without removing the lie. John 8:36 states: *"If the Son sets you free, you will be free indeed."* When Jesus is invited into that place of wounding where the lie began and He ministers His truth, lasting change does come.

Chapter Two

# PURPOSE FOR WRITING BOOK

One purpose for writing this book is to emphasize the fact that Jesus came to save us from more than hell. He also came to save us from ourselves. In Luke 4:18–21, Jesus stood in the synagogue and read from a passage in Isaiah (chapter 61) stating what the Messiah was coming to do. He said that He was coming to bind up or heal the brokenhearted, proclaim freedom and release for prisoners from darkness, *"recovery of sight for the blind, to release the oppressed, [and] to proclaim the year of the Lord's favor."* Wow! Who feels more like a misfit than those who are broken and wounded, those imprisoned in darkness, and those who are spiritually blind and oppressed? Or Christians who live with guilt, feel they aren't good enough, and are afraid they are falling short of what God expects of them.

When Jesus finished reading, He said, *"Today this scripture is fulfilled in your hearing."* He was making the public declaration that He was the promised One who had come to preach good news to the poor, the good news that He came to do everything that He had just read from Isaiah. When you are poor or lacking in any area of your life, it is great news to know that God has already made provision for your needs. In life we can live without a nice house or without enough food on our table, but

7

we cannot successfully live up to all God desires for us when we struggle with sin, have emotional pain, or don't feel good about who we are. John tells us in 3 John 2, *"I pray that you may enjoy good health and that all may go well with you, even as your soul is getting along well"* . . . or prospers. So many of us are emotional and spiritual cripples, and that is like trying to swim the sea of life with a cement block chained to our foot.

When I taught in the county jail, I told the women that we are held captive in our hearts far more than by the bars that hold them. The passage of time will release most physical prisoners, but those of us who need freedom from painful experiences cannot just walk out of them because the calendar says it's time. Whoever said that time heals all wounds certainly didn't speak the truth. Each of us have places inside that need to be set free from pain, feelings of rejection or offense, having been neglected or betrayed, and feelings of abandonment or not being loved. We have places where we are blind and need our vision restored. God knew that we would be wounded by others and life. From the beginning He had a plan that could remove our pain and allow us to live a peaceful, prosperous, and joyous life. Jesus is that plan.

Hebrews 9:13–14 tells us that the blood of animals sanctified the people so that they were outwardly clean, but the blood of Christ will *"cleanse our consciences from acts that lead to death, so that we may serve the living God."* When you have a spill of some kind and wipe it up, it's making the surface outwardly clean. In some cases, that is all that seems to be required. But when you spill something that has a dye in it, it requires a cleansing that will penetrate and remove the stain. I've not met one person who doesn't have a "spill" of some kind inside of them in the form of a hurt or disappointment from experiences in life. When a wound has penetrated the spirit, heart, or soul of a person, wiping off the surface (forgiving) is not always sufficient to remove the pain.

I am not discounting the importance of forgiveness. It is a powerful tool in the hands of a Christian. Forgiveness is a requirement of the Lord (Mark 11:25), and forgiving unties God's hands and allows Him to work in a situation. We know that forgiveness does not remove the guilt of the one who did the wounding, but it does release the heart of the hurt one to begin the healing process. Those wounded places inside of us, experiences that we can't seem to get over, the disappointment or anger that gnaws at us, or the rejection we feel are part of the "acts that lead to death" (Hebrews 9:14). Emotional struggles and spiritual death will, at the very least, hinder your Christian walk and growth. When Jesus is invited into that place of wounding, you will begin to experience a release from the pain. Only Jesus and His blood can do the deep cleansing and healing we need to be released from that inner prison. No wonder it is called precious blood.

My second purpose for this book is to let you know that there ARE reasons why we feel miss fit in life, and none of them are impossible to overcome. I want you to know a Jesus that loves you so much that He took upon Himself on the cross EVERYTHING that you have experienced or could experience so that His precious blood could cover it all. Hebrews 12:2 tells us that Jesus endured the cross because of the joy set before Him. He made the ultimate sacrifice with joyous expectation of the freedom He was purchasing for us. WOW! A Jesus who can save us from ourselves!

Third, I will give you spiritual principles from the Word that hold beliefs captive in our hearts. I want to give you an understanding of how our early life experiences (from the moment of conception) set the stage for beliefs about ourselves, others, and life. You will see why general prayers like "God, please take away my pain," or "God, if I have any anger, please take it away," are not effective. I believe you will finish this book by saying, "Now I know why I . . ." and I will finish by saying, "Praise God!"

Ultimately, my purpose is not just to be informational, but transformational. Jesus didn't come to earth to give us more religious information. He came to change lives. If Christianity really works (and it does), it is not good enough just to know how to cope with our unfit feelings, learn a better limp, or discover a different distraction from our pain. We need Jesus to do for us what He is so good at doing—heal our broken hearts and set us free.

When our lives are producing ungodly fruit, we need to know how to get that to stop. Spiritual fruit has spiritual roots, and spiritual roots have spiritual seeds, simple as that; spiritual seeds need spiritual redemption. We need to understand and recognize how the seeds we planted in our hearts have produced fruit in our lives that is hindering us from being all that God wants us to be and from living victorious lives. And we need to understand that just plucking the fruit off the tree (stopping the behavior, thoughts, sin, etc.) is not dealing with the real problem, just the symptoms—the resultant thoughts and behaviors. Just an acorn doesn't grow into a maple tree, and anger and resentment don't produce peace and wholeness, so the negative seeds we've sown into our hearts cannot produce godly fruit (Matthew 12:33). Stopping our bad behavior—as good as that is to do—without dealing with reason that is producing the unwanted behavior, is like picking all the fruit off a tree and believing all future harvests are over. When Jesus is invited to minister His truth to our sinful seed, we can experience the reality of John 8:32, *"Then you will know the truth, and the truth will set you free."* I have experienced John 8:36—the Son setting me free, and I'm free indeed!

Chapter Three

# SPIRITUAL LAWS
# OF GOD

Before man ever existed, God established spiritual principles that are absolute and eternal. He is a God of order, and when the laws He created that govern the natural and spiritual realms are broken, it sets their consequences into motion. Unbelief, disbelief, or ignorance of them does not nullify their power or cause them not to be activated. Just as the natural law of gravity is the same for everyone, God's spiritual laws are also all-encompassing; no one or anything can escape them. Part of the good news of the Gospel is that when we repent and ask God to forgive us, we can be released from continuing to reap those spiritual consequences.

**Sowing and Reaping:**
This is probably the foundational spiritual law, as it seems to encompass all the others. Galatians 6:7 says that we WILL reap what we sow. Farmers and gardeners are glad for that; we who plant seeds of "less than godly things" in our hearts aren't quite so grateful. A farmer would think it foolish to plant corn seed and expect a harvest of green beans. Why would we think that we could plant a seed of resentment or anger in our hearts and not have it grow and produce after its own kind? As we

experience hurtful events or situations that seem to call for our judgment, no matter what our age, the seeds we plant in our hearts begin their spiritual process of taking root, growing stronger and bearing fruit. Once a seed is sown, it is established. Everything we choose to believe about ourselves, others, life, and God are directional signposts in our lives. And when those beliefs are conceived in pain, fear, or anger, they are not usually choices that are helpful to our emotional or spiritual growth or development. Even though we may not remember making them, our judgments are still there, and we will reap the consequences. Everything in our lives that is rooted and birthed in sin will produce a harvest of unrighteousness. God's Word holds true whether we understand it or not. I had a friend ask me why God would hold a person responsible for planting something in his heart when he doesn't remember it or didn't realize what he was doing. The answer is the spiritual law of sowing and reaping. The statement that "Ignorance of the law is no excuse" holds true also in the spiritual realm. Our lives clearly live out the truth of Matthew 12:33, *"Make a tree good and its fruit will be good, or make a tree bad and its fruit will be bad, for a tree is recognized by its fruit."*

In addition to our own lies and judgments, wrong beliefs are presented to us by others, whether it is intentional or by lifestyle. I remember being in a store and from the next aisle hearing a dad say to his young son, "Men never ask directions." That dad was not trying to give his son poor advice. But for whatever reasons, it was truth as he believed it, and he was passing it on to his impressionable child. Unfortunately, many of the "truths" we learn or choose to believe are detrimental to our emotional well-being, our success in life, and our spiritual growth, because they are not in agreement with the Word of God. When we take the defensive posture that our parents "did the best they could," we may bring an understanding to what previously didn't make any sense, but it DOES NOT bring healing to those old wounds or nullify your judgments, and certainly does not stop the reaping in our lives.

Hebrews 12:15 tells us, *"See to it that no one misses the grace of God and that no bitter root grows up to cause trouble and defile many."* By virtue of what the Word says here, a bitter root will grow—gain strength and get bigger, causing trouble and bringing defilement to more than just that person. A bitter root can be resentment, anger, unforgiveness, a lie we choose to believe, a promise we make to ourselves that is based in some form of judgment against someone, or our reaction to rejection or an unmet need. They are bitter because they were rooted in pain, anger, or in a resentful attitude. I knew a woman who was exceptionally angry at abortionists and at the women who chose to end their pregnancies. She had absolutely no compassion or tolerance for any of it. In my wonderings of why she was so adamant, I found out that she was barren. Her hurt and resentment at her inability to bear children were so immense that she allowed her heart to be filled with anger, hatred, and bitterness.

**Judging others:**

Matthew 7:1–2 says, *"Do not judge, or you too will be judged. For in the same way you judge others, you will be judged, and with the measure you use, it will be measured to you."* And Romans 2:1 tells us, *"You, therefore, have no excuse, you who pass judgment on someone else, for at whatever point you judge the other, you are condemning yourself, because you who pass judgment do the same things."* It is natural to be upset or angry when someone does something that hurts us. Our problem is in holding on to that anger and resentful attitude. As children we don't usually have an adult who is able to effectively help us deal with our anger or pain. It seems we are often told, "Go to your room until you can stop being angry"; told we shouldn't be angry about that—they didn't mean it, it was an accident; or, "Stop crying, that didn't hurt!" Instead of releasing our anger and resentment, we push it down and hide it so we are again socially acceptable. When a child's feelings (whether they seem right or wrong) are not validated, it feels like no one cares he is hurt.

An example of Romans 2:1 might be a child whose mother was a screamer or yeller. The child hated it so much that in her resentment and anger, she promised herself that she would never yell at her kids like her mother yelled at her. While her decision to not hurt her children as she had been hurt was a good one, because she made that promise to herself in the midst of pain, resentment, and anger at her mother, her good desire was defiled. Whether or not she went through life remembering her vow and judgment against her mother, one day it turned against her as she began reaping what she had sown many years before, and she found herself doing what she had hated.

A young girl could angrily promise herself that she will never marry a man who will mistreat her children like she was abused. She may resentfully vow that she will never marry a man like her mother married. Unfortunately, in the spirit realm, the consequences of judgments like that very often will draw her to an angry or critical man or one who doesn't respect or value women or children. And if she has a childhood expectation of that type of behavior from men, that expectation also is a spiritual draw for that behavior. It's difficult to understand why many women (or men) are repeatedly drawn to people who do what they hated and vowed against. It is possible that they are reaping from the anger, judgments, vows, and bitter expectations they sowed into their hearts in the midst of their pain.

My son is a prime example of judging something and living

out the results of a bitter root expectation. As a teen his cars were less than wonderful. On an out-of-state trip as a young adult, his car took the ultimate death leap and decided to not live again. Not only was his wonderfully planned weekend ruined, he was far from home and far from his destination. He had to figure out what to do with his expired vehicle and then how to get home. In disappointment and anger over his used cars, he promised himself that he would never buy another used car. After returning home, he purchased a new vehicle and was proudly enjoying his fine, new ride. A few hours after driving it off the car lot, he backed into a snow bank and broke a taillight. He was very angry. A few days later he was helping a friend move, and as he pushed her furniture into the back hatch, he tore the roof lining. Needless to say, he was livid! I approached him gingerly and said, "I think I know what is going on. Would you like me to tell you?" He agreed to listen. I asked him if he had ever thought or said, "Every car I ever have will have something wrong with it!" Indeed, he had. I explained that when we believe and make a statement like that, it sets our bitter expectation into motion in the spirit realm, and his new car had no choice but to fulfill his angry expectation and belief. He repented of his anger, asked God to forgive him for his judgment and expectation, and we broke the power of them in Jesus' name. Praise God, the reaping stopped. Unfortunately, not all of our judgmental lessons are learned so easily.

When we feel anger rise up within us, choose not to nurse or embrace it, and ask God's forgiveness, I believe we are living out Ephesians 4:26, *"In your anger do not sin."* The ability to state the truth about someone or something and do it without anger, accusation, or hurtful emotions is not judging. Judgment is in our critical attitude toward the person or situation; it is a heart condition.

**Honor/dishonor parents:**

God was very specific when He told Moses to write the Ten Commandments. He clearly stated the consequences (reaping) in Deuteronomy 5:16, *"Honor your father and your mother, as the Lord your God has commanded you, so that you may live long and that it may go well with you."* The Lord then adds in Ephesians 6:2–3, *"'Honor your father and mother'—which is the first commandment with a promise—that it may go well with you and that you may enjoy long life on the earth."* It's easy to only focus on the first half of those verses. But the reality of what we will reap if we don't honor our parents is clearly presented. So, in those areas where you honor/respect your parents, God says it will go well for you. But you will have difficulty in whatever areas you dishonor/judge them.

Often, adults are reluctant to tell the failures and sins of their parents because they think it is dishonoring them. Dishonor is a matter of the heart and attitude, not stating the facts. When we judge our parents as lacking in ability or decision-making, if we are critical about particular areas of their lives, or when we are resentful and angry over things that happened or didn't happen, we have stepped over the line of honoring them. Honor doesn't imply that what they did was right. Honor does not mean you are not hurt. Honor is knowing what they did, not holding it against them, and keeping your heart pure before the Lord concerning the issue.

Even when parents (or others) commit grievous sins against us, we need to get to the place where we can forgive and release them. For some, that can't happen until they experience an intervention from the Lord. A young woman told me about a very hurtful thing her mother had done to her which was still continuing in her life. Even though she knew she needed to forgive and wanted to on a conscious level, her severely wounded heart would not allow her to do it. As we prayed, I asked the Lord to lift off the disappointment of the rejection she felt from her mother. Amazingly, she immediately said, "I want to forgive her."

People are often surprised when they come to the understanding that holding an offense against a parent (no matter how early in life it happened) does not allow them to move beyond the hurt or fully mature in that area of their lives. Many times they can't recognize or receive love when it is offered. A young woman recognized that as a little girl she had angrily blamed her dad for hurting her mother and being verbally and mentally abusive. She recounted the nice things her dad did for her as a child. Even though he took her for ice cream and to the mall, she couldn't see beyond her angry, critical judgment that he was doing these things because he felt guilty or was trying to get on her good side. There wasn't any way she was able to receive the love he offered. In fact, she became more resentful because of his efforts. I remember the day she recognized that holding those offenses and anger against her father blinded her from seeing and recognizing her own heart issues/sin. In her adult life, whenever she encountered a situation that felt like the ones in early life with her dad, she immediately rose up in anger against that person, letting him know exactly what she felt and thought. She felt justified for that behavior because she was determined that no one would ever treat her like that again and get away with it. When a current situation touched her old pain and judgments, she went into action. In prayer she forgave her dad and released the offenses she held in her heart against him. She repented and asked God to forgive her for her anger, blame, and judgments. Then, we invited Jesus to come and take the anger and blame and heal her heart. The change in her was instant and tremendous. She was then able to embrace her father, tell him that she loved him, and receive his love. In fact, the timing of God's redemption in her heart was so perfect that, soon after, her father moved into her home, and she was able to lovingly care for him until his death. There is no one or anything that can transform a life like that other than Jesus.

One way to recognize if you have dishonored your parents is to observe if you struggle in an area of life in which you did not like their actions, or if you are doing that which you resented them doing. To speak practically about Ephesians 6, if you dishonor your parents in the arena of finances, you can be sure that you will have a seat in that same arena. Your problem may not be exactly the same, but most likely you will struggle with financial issues in some way. When you dishonor your parents concerning rules or boundaries, you most likely will have struggles in that area of your life; if not with yourself, then probably with your children, and very possibly with God. We can't expect life to go well for us in any area where we hold dishonor.

If you judged your dad to be weak, for whatever reason, your judgment will often draw that type of person to you. The weakness may be in a different area, but you will very likely end up marrying someone who in some way fits the description of what you hated and vowed against. If you resentfully judged your mother for marrying someone who was weak and promised yourself you would never do that, the spiritual magnet you created and its consequences may be stronger than your desire to not do it.

Many of the consequences of our dishonoring don't become active in our lives until we get married. If your judgment was concerning something within your parents' marriage, you may not reap the result while you are single. Marriage is a spiritual contract, and once you enter into that agreement, your judgments involving marriage have a spiritually legal place to operate.

I've thought it would be interesting to teach a class on "Why I Married My Dad" (or Mother). Often people say their spouse is just like their father or mother, and they are NOT pleased about it. Dishonoring parents is probably the biggest culprit. This commandment's promise is one of the reasons why it seems that a person changes after marriage. I've heard story after story about couples who had a long-term relationship or lived together, and as soon as they got married, one of them seemed to change. The consequences of their judgment/dishonoring finally had a spiritual place to operate in their lives. I know of a case where the judgments and resentment were against her brothers, and when she married, those judgments became spiritually active, and she felt her spouse was doing the same.

A child who hears his dad complaining about his wife nagging at him can also become resentful about it. He may decide that his mother nags at him too, and hates it. It would be easy for him to develop a lifestyle of believing women are naggers. He probably will have difficulty listening to female teachers and may struggle with a woman boss. Later in life, when his own wife tries to tell him something, even when she does it in a loving or noncondemning manner, he most likely will rise up against it because it feels too much like his childhood; it's like he hears his mother's voice through his wife's voice. The truth is that he is hearing through his own hurts, judgments, and vows.

When a child experiences pain because of his parents' marital troubles (especially if it keeps repeating itself), in his hurt and frustration he may begin to believe that that is how it will always be. Any time we expect or believe something is going to happen, it is like faith working in our lives; faith works, even when it is about something negative. I ministered to a man who feared his wife was going to leave him. Even though she hadn't given any indication of wanting to leave, he couldn't shake that gnawing feeling inside him. We asked the Lord to remind him of the first time he felt abandoned; it was when he was young and he saw his dad drive away and never return. As that young boy, he began an expectation of being abandoned, and now it was manifesting in his current marriage. If we would have only asked God to help him not be afraid his wife was going to leave him or asked his wife for confirmation that she didn't intend to leave, we would never have gotten to the real cause of his fear. After the Lord healed his wound of abandonment (it's like a "little boy" part of him was still grieving and fearful of being alone), the fear of his wife leaving was gone without our having to deal with it. We can establish a belief or fear of what will happen based on our experience, anger, resentment, or pain.

I knew a young woman who had a bitter root expectation that men will get you pregnant and then leave you. That was her childhood experience as her dad left home when her mom was pregnant with the next child. Through her mother's hurt and anger, my guess is that that bitter root was reinforced verbally as she grew up. As a teen she became pregnant, and sure enough, her expectation became a reality. She, then, altered her belief to specify that men of your own race will get you pregnant and then leave you. She continued through many more pregnancies, each absent father being a different nationality.

**The wages of sin is death:**

Another spiritual law is the payment for sin. Romans 6:23 states that *"the wages of sin is death."* We know that we will ultimately face eternal death unless we accept Jesus as our Savior—the only One who could pay for and remove our sins. But we experience a death in our spiritual life also as a result of sin. One time I went to my pastor and said that I was having a difficult time praying, reading the Bible, etc. He wisely asked what had recently happened in my life; what was it that seemed to turn my heart away? I discovered that disappointment, guilt, shame, anger, and unforgiveness are powerful spiritual stranglers. Some of us never mature spiritually because of our early life heart issues. There is always a payment for sin. Sin always separates: you from me, and us from God.

# Chapter Four

# A PERSON WHO FEELS LIKE A MISFIT NEEDS TO KNOW THAT . . .

. . . there are valid reasons for feeling like you do and believing what you believe. As you read on, I believe you will begin to understand some of the "whys" and "how comes" of your life and that it will be a relief to you when you come to realize that you are not a misfit or weird, just wounded.

. . . when you say, "I've always felt this way," or "I was born this way," I understand and believe you. But please don't buy into the lie, "This is the way God made me." God doesn't create misfits, and it isn't His desire for you to feel like one. There are explainable reasons why you were born feeling like you do. Most of us don't know the circumstances around which we were conceived, but I can tell you by the experiences of many that our conception and the reaction of our parents when they first discovered they were pregnant has a profound effect on who we think we are and how we relate to life. I say "who you think you are" because it may not be your true identity as God sees and knows you, but it is "truth" as you feel it. When the truth we believe doesn't line up with the Word of God, it may be our reaction to hurtful situations. In the midst of rejection or traumatic events, we choose something to believe, and many times it is about ourselves.

. . . each of us begins to form our identity as we experience acceptance or rejection in the first weeks and months of our lives. Our time in the womb has as profound an influence on us as anything else that can happen to us in life. All of us are born ALREADY BELIEVING things about ourselves, others, and life. Fortunately, if your time in the womb was peaceful, and your parents were pleased and excited you were there, you were born with an inner knowing that you were wanted and loved and a sense of security about who you are. If your mother's womb was not a friendly place where you felt safe, wanted, and accepted, you were probably born already not liking yourself. In later chapters I will give specifics on how that happens. The psalmist David said in Psalm 51:5–6, *"Surely I was sinful at birth, sinful from the time my mother conceived me. Surely you desire truth in the inner parts; you teach me wisdom in the inmost place."* It appears that David was saying he was sinful at birth; we can and do sin while in the womb. I know a man whom the Lord gave a spiritual picture of himself being born. The Lord showed him "spread eagle" and screaming "NOOO!" If that's not rebellion or fear from the womb, I don't know what is! His life continued with the complications of that wounding, rebellion, and fear.

. . . God is the standard for truth. I have a friend that needed an understanding about truth. The Lord gave him a picture of God's truth as a strong tower, and no matter what lies he hurled at it, it didn't mar or alter God's truth in the least; it never changed. So it is with us. No matter what we believe, whether it was from the womb or later in life, whether we believe it silently or scream it, it does not change God's truth about us. You won't find anything in the Word of God that tells us that He created some of us good and some as misfits. The old saying that "God doesn't make junk" is absolutely true. But the truth in your heart will always take precedence over your biblical knowledge, because you believe it based it on your experience. Just as my friend had his reasons for screaming "NOOO!" about being born, we also have reasons why we believe what we do about ourselves. The really good news is that Jesus doesn't have any problem reaching back into our place of pain and ministering His truth. It is so amazing to watch the transformation in a person's life when the Lord gives His truth to the individual, and the ungodly belief is gone.

. . . everything about Jesus is hope. Part of the good news of the Bible is Jesus wanting to touch our places of pain. Only a God of relationship would care that we hurt and would make provision for our healing and wholeness. Whether our spiritual eyesight is blurred by emotional scars or lies we believe about ourselves, others, life, or God, those things darken our ability to see God's truth.

Imagine a stack of colored cellophane in graduating colors— the lightest colors representing less painful life events, darker colors for more severe things that happen to us, and very dark colors for the offenses against us that have the most impact and change in our lives. Now, put one layer of each appropriate color of cellophane for each event in your life over your eyes. That is how we see and live life—through the color of our experiences and beliefs. The appropriate questions for us should be: 1) God, where or how is my vision obstructed, or where am I blinded? (Not, am I blind in some way?) 2) God, how or where am I held captive? (Not, am I being held captive?) I can guarantee that no one is totally free from lies, but praise God, the more healing we receive, the more of God's truths we can fully believe.

. . . no matter how long you have felt like a misfit, there are reasons, and there are spiritual solutions.

Chapter Five

# GOING TO THE ROOTS

Sometimes we ask the question, why do we need to dig up the past? After all, what's happened is done and over with; we can't change the past. I agree that while our history is firmly set in place, the pain we carry, judgments, defiled promises to ourselves, anger, hatred, etc., and our resultant beliefs and behaviors ARE redeemable by the Lord. When Jesus said He came to heal the brokenhearted, it only makes sense that we have to go to the place of brokenness for that to happen. If your teapot falls and the handle breaks off, it won't do any good to polish the pot or put glue on the spout. The broken place needs to be mended. Fortunately for us, we can go back in prayer; Jesus knows no limitation of time and events. Like a weed that you want out of your yard, you have to get the root, or it will raise its ugly head again.

It seems to be in our Christian nature, when anger or some other nasty issue surfaces, to pray and ask God to help us not feel that way or ask Him to take away our wrong feelings. Our desire is right, but prayers like that are like asking God to sweep it under the rug. That may be appropriate for the moment when the situation needs to be defused or your emotions need to be calmed. God, in His grace, may cause whatever is happening to subside and the person to feel relieved. Once the thoughts or feelings lessen or stop, there is a tendency to believe the issue has been resolved. The truth is that the emotion of the moment has lifted, but until the root is exposed and dealt with, the problem is still there under the rug waiting for it to be kicked up again.

Our past, even if it is not in our conscious memory, has a powerful influence on who we are (or think we are), what we do, and what we believe. Our wounded places, no matter how early in life they happened or how deeply we have buried them, are like rivers flowing beneath the surface. Some are only a trickle or creek, but some are a substantial river with lots of stuff and power in them. That little root of bitterness that may have seemed justified or innocent, unless the grace of God intervenes, will grow up to cause trouble and defile many (Hebrews 12:15). Sin can only beget (birth/produce) sin. That little puddle of resentment or anger that you started out with very likely will increase to the size of a lake, and its water will be even more polluted.

Many people experience the spiritual principle that Hosea spoke about in Hosea 8:7, *"They sow the wind and reap the whirlwind."* The scriptural principle of increase can be very destructive when it empowers our sin. Even though those little seeds we planted in our hearts may seem insignificant or powerless, they are always a breeding ground of sin.

As those toxic rivers continue to flow within us, they will splash up their spiritual poisons from time to time, and will occasionally, overflow their banks and cause an ungodly disturbance around them. When our hearts hold unforgiveness, anger, or judgments, we are like a well whose water is polluted. Proverbs 4:23 reads, *"Above all else, guard your heart, for it is the wellspring of life."* Everyone who is touched by that water receives some of its defilement, but the person who "owns" the polluted well drinks daily from it.

Christians are often so concerned about stopping their

outward behaviors that they rarely search for the roots or causes of them. Usually, we consider the battle won and raise the victory flag when we overcome a bad habit or sinful behavior. While self-control is definite reason for celebration, if it continues to take a constant effort to keep up the good behavior or you have to continually resist temptation, it is not a completed victory. To constantly have to "try not to think about it" is not victorious living. We tend to think the fruit we are producing in our lives (our thoughts, behaviors, addictions, sins, etc.) is the problem. While those things are a problem, they are not the problem. They are only the symptoms or resultant behaviors, the fruit.

In harvest season after all the apples are picked from a tree, it continues to live, grow, and produce again at the next season. Our spiritual fruit is the same. As long as we just stop our "bad acts" (plucking the fruit) and don't deal with the roots and reasons for producing ungodly fruit, it won't be long before the next crop is ripe and ready. When the underlying heart issue is dealt with, the outward actions change because the inner need or drive that produces that fruit is eliminated. That's why our New Year's resolutions of choosing to change or make better choices don't always work. Our behaviors can be driven from within us. Once the inner "want to" or "need to" is gone, the victory banner can be firmly planted as a testament to the freeing power of Jesus.

I know a woman who was trying to stop swearing and using foul language; it was a regular part of her conversations. It took a constant effort to try to change; instead of getting better, it got worse. We asked the Lord to show her where or when she started swearing so we could deal with the root. The Lord reminded her of when she was about eleven years old, and she and her mother moved into her uncle's house. Even though financially she and the other children were provided for, she felt responsible for childcare, cleaning, cooking, and shopping. Her way of dealing with that stress as a young girl was to release her anger and frustration verbally. As an adult, every time she was under stress, her language took on a new intensity. She repented and asked God to forgive her. We asked Jesus to lift off the stress she felt as a young girl and minister His healing. Her language instantly changed for the better. Praise God! It was Jesus doing just what He said He came to do.

Many times we don't recognize or realize we have toxic rivers flowing within us until we experience their overflow. For some, it's like the toxic water rises until it has to overflow its boundaries, causing its poisons to damage whatever it touches. For others, it's like a tsunami and destroys everything in its path. We can be blindsided about our "attitude" because we've grown accustomed to it; many times we have had it since birth or very young childhood. It seems to be human nature to think it's the other person's problem. Some proudly wear a tee shirt that says, "It's MY attitude—deal with it!" It's easy to believe our predominant attitude in life is part of our personality—and if it's part of our personality, then it must be how God made us. God did not design or create any of us fearful, angry, defeated, depressed, or as a misfit. I can say with confidence that if your attitude is less than godly, it was not part of God's original design.

A volcano that has been dormant for decades can suddenly erupt for no apparent reason. But, please understand, there is ALWAYS an underlying reason when we suddenly become enraged, when we generate far more anger than the current situation would seem to merit, or when we are far more offended than seems appropriate. Road rage is evidence of much deeper anger than traffic situations. People say they are thin-skinned. If that's the case, there are reasons for it. Your arm doesn't hurt when it's touched unless it already has a bruise. The right situation can trigger our seemingly inactive volcano into a current event. Once the spewing starts, there isn't much to do but damage control. One day when my children were in young grade school, they were standing in the doorway of the kitchen. I didn't know what triggered me, but I found myself in an angry fit. I knew enough NOT to touch them, so I took two dining room chairs and smashed them against the floor until they were in as many pieces as I could get them. Believe me, I was as shocked as my children were. I had no conscious clue that I held that much anger and rage. After all, I'd been saved since I was twelve years old and had always faithfully loved and served God. I knew nothing else to do but push the anger back inside. Back then, I didn't want to tell anyone and "air my dirty laundry" when I didn't know a way to clean it.

Even if your inner rivers never get out of control, their polluted water will always contaminate everything it touches (Hebrews 12:15). Proverbs 27:19 states, *"As water reflects a face, so a man's heart reflects the man."* Calm waters reflect an image from above, but water that is contaminated with anger, unforgiveness, resentment, and offense can only reflect the heart from which it flows. When our emotional "waters" are troubled, it isn't possible to have a clear reflection of God from above. We need to cry out like the psalmist did in Psalm 51:10, *"Create in me a pure heart, O God, and renew a steadfast spirit within me."*

Some believe they are a stronger person (and even give God the credit) for their ability to keep their anger and rage under control. While it is better to restrain yourself than display your anger or rage through behaviors, it's hard to imagine our God endorsing the belief that harboring the sin in your heart is a good thing.

No matter how much of our history we've tried to forget or ignore, until the Lord goes into that place of wounding, the pain remains and the river flows. One time I was praying for a woman, and we were dealing with abandonment issues. She told me that her birth father had left the home when she was just an infant and that she had never known him. She insisted that his leaving didn't have any lasting effect on her because she had never known him. I asked if I could invite Jesus into that place in her that was abandoned by her father. She agreed, and to her amazement there was much pain there—until Jesus arrived!

# Chapter Six

# ROOTS AND REASONS

Imagine beginning life believing you are shameful or not wanted, feeling you are the cause of family problems, or knowing you can never measure up to your parents' expectations. That child will find it difficult to fully embrace life with all its wonderful possibilities and will experience some level of poor self-esteem. Although the belief that an embryo is a baby and a viable life is not popular with many people, I am convinced beyond a shadow of a doubt that babies just conceived and beginning to form in the womb are a valuable life complete with a human spirit (Zechariah 12:1). Life begins at the moment of conception, not at birth. An unborn child knows when he is wanted and loved or when things are not good and he doesn't feel safe. The experience of being joyously received by our expectant parents or feeling the rejection, anger, shame, or guilt from parents that DID NOT want to be pregnant immediately sets us up on the stage of life already deciding what role we will play in the cast of characters.

Job 32:8–9 says, *"It is the spirit in a man, the breath of the Almighty, that gives him understanding. It is not only the old who are wise, not only the aged who understand what is right."* Even though an embryo, fetus, or young child is not able to cognitively understand right from wrong or good from evil because his brain is not fully developed, his human spirit has that awareness and does know whether something is good or bad. The baby in the womb is well aware of conflicts, fears, rejection, etc., and love and acceptance. While praying for the man who had the spiritual picture of himself screaming "NOOO!" about being born, the Lord showed me his dad pointing at his pregnant wife and venomously saying, "I hate you and I hate that baby." It is no wonder that he didn't want to come into the realities of his world; he was already fearful of what life would be like. By the time we are born, the first layer of our foundation has been set in place.

Parents are supposed to be a reflection of God's nature to their children. Through their words and actions to their children, parents should be a human demonstration of God's delight with them and unconditional love. Unconditional love does not mean that everything the child does is right, but demonstrates love and acceptance of the child, no matter what happens or what he does; it allows the child to know he is good even if what he did is not good. Children who feel loved, honored, and respected by their parents generally can more easily experience a positive connection with God as an adult. Each of us can only live life and parent out of our own woundedness; we react through the grid of our own experiences, value of life, anger, fears, pain, and limitations. I vividly remember the day I asked my adult son to forgive me. I told him, "Yesterday I believed I was one of the best mothers in the world, but today I believe I am one of the worst." It was a couple weeks before I was at peace with that realization. One day I sensed the Lord telling me that if I had had a floodlight to live by, I would have used it. I was so grateful that the Lord settled my heart with that perspective.

Children who live with rejection, neglect, or abuse of any kind feel devalued. It doesn't matter if a child experiences it in the womb or during childhood, the effects are powerful in the formation of who they believe they are and if they have any value. A child in the womb who "witnesses" or experiences his mother being abused usually takes it very personally—many times believing if he wasn't there, Mommy wouldn't be hurt. That is a heavy burden for a child to bear, and it usually results in guilt or shame, anger, and self-hatred. I believe if we could literally see the roots of diseases where our body fights against or attacks itself, we would find many of them connected to anger at self and self-hatred. If I believed I didn't have any value, if I believed I shouldn't have been born, or if I felt responsible for someone else's pain or troubles, why wouldn't I hate myself?

Our experiences in the early years of our lives lay the next layer of foundation of who we believe we are. A child born already believing he's a mistake and his existence is wrong may shrink back and try to hide behind his shame; he may behave in a way that will try to prove you are correct in believing he's not good or valuable; he may be oversensitive, feeling correction means he is not good enough; or he's going to do everything he can to prove you wrong by being the best little boy in the world. He may become an overachiever to win the approval of those around him in an effort to prove he is good and has a right to exist.

Many times words were spoken about us or to us that have crippled us from moving beyond the judgmental power and expectation that those words hold. I remember hearing John Sandford, founder of Elijah House, say that for a person to not become or do what someone's bitter root expectation declares would be like trying to walk into a gale-force wind. Our angry, judgmental, and critical expectations can stop a person from becoming anything other than what we have judged them to be or do. So many children are told they are worthless or will never amount to anything, and they live their lives trying to put truth to those words or prove them wrong. I had an interesting experience many years ago. My pastor had visited some friends we had both known in past years. As he was relating what he said to them, he said, "Sue is a woman of God." When I heard the word "woman," it felt really strange to me—like it didn't fit. As I examined those feelings and their possible roots, I came to the conclusion that as a child someone had said to me, "You will never grow up," and it landed painfully in my heart because it would have been spoken out of some form of frustration or dislike. Possibly there was some point in childhood when I decided I didn't want to grow up; I didn't want to become a woman. I forgave anyone I thought could have said that to me and asked God to forgive me for believing it and not wanting to grow up. Then we broke the power of those words in Jesus' name. From that time on, describing myself as a woman has felt comfortable.

Every baby in the womb, every infant, and every child NEEDS affectionate touch, nurture, and affirmation from his parents to help establish a solid foundation for his life. Affectionate touch meets emotional needs and helps to establish self-worth within a child. It communicates the parents' love, concern, and care for his needs, and acceptance of him. When parents nurture their child, letting him know how valuable he is to them through their words and actions, a sense of value is instilled within him. Nurture touches the human spirit, the very essence of our being.

Affirmation is vital to a child's emotional well-being, because through it he is acknowledged as a person of worth and importance. I remember the impact it had on me the day I witnessed my nephew-in-law putting his affirmation into action. He was in an adult conversation when one of his young children came up to him. He turned from that conversation to warmly embrace his child and see what the need was. Many of us would have "put our child off" by telling him to wait until we were done. He demonstrated his love by having "bright eyes" for his child—eyes that light up when you walk in; eyes that say, "I love you, I receive you, and I embrace you." How would most of our lives have been different if we would have had parents or other significant people who we felt had bright eyes for us? To feel lovingly and warmly received—no matter what else is happening or what you did—is vital to a good self-image. No wonder so many people, even Christians, have a difficult time believing God has "bright eyes" for them.

When a child is affirmed as valuable, he has an inner knowing that he is good and acceptable. He will be able to distinguish between having a failure and being a failure; what a security that offers to a child. When these loving attributes are not given to a child, his self-value is lessened. We are able to realize the devastating effects that abuse has on an individual, but we don't always recognize that an infant or child also feels devalued when he senses rejection or his needs are not met. Meeting the "well-being" needs of a child are far more important to his beliefs of who he is and if he has value than meeting physical needs of clothing, housing, etc. A child can feel good about himself without top-of-the-line clothing or a fabulous house, but he will not have an inner sense of his goodness if it can only come from what he has or does. I have a clear recollection of the pictures I saw as an adolescent of an emaciated, deformed young woman who had been shut away in an attic all her life, never touched or cared for, only given food. I remember how it tore my heart, and I was horrified by the physical effect that neglect had had upon her. Now that I understand spiritual things, my spirit grieves for what she experienced. One of my heart passions is to minister to innocent victims. Innocent victims—that is exactly what we are when we experience neglect, rejection, abuse, or are a victim of someone else's actions. Jesus died to heal the broken hearts of all victims.

When a child experiences verbal, emotional, physical, mental, or sexual abuse, any sense of value he did have will be stripped away. It is very easy for him to come to the conclusion that "There must be something wrong with me." Because it's usually a "hushed" situation, many children believe they are the only ones being abused—so it must be their fault; they deserve it because they aren't lovable or valuable, or are bad. A child can shut down emotionally or become overly aggressive when he is neglected, ridiculed, belittled, shamed, rejected, or provoked. A child who believes he doesn't have any value often won't value life in others. He often produces behaviors that are not safe or socially acceptable.

Biblical truth about the value of God's children and how important we are to Him can't fully penetrate a heart that felt rejected or devalued very early in life. That's why it's easier to believe God's truth for someone else and not for yourself; you know they are valuable. We are quick to believe that it is the devil who is telling us that we are worthless or a failure, when in actuality, very likely those thoughts are coming from within our own hearts. The New American Standard Bible states Matthew 12:34 this way: *"For the mouth speaks out of that which fills the heart."* I would paraphrase: Our thoughts come from that which fills our heart, and our mouth speaks it out. The devil does try to deceive, discourage, and attack us by telling us lies and accusing us, but if it's easy to be in agreement with what you think he is telling you, I suggest you examine your heart for the root of the belief.

# Chapter Seven

# MORE EXAMPLES OF ROOTS AND REASONS

### Generational inheritance:

Another powerful root in our lives is generational sin. Our culture understands the importance of heredity; the medical field is intently interested in family history of disease. However, many do not understand the spiritual significance of generational issues. Exodus 34:7 states, *"Visiting the iniquity of the fathers upon the children, and upon the children's children, unto the third and to the fourth generation"* (King James Version). Recently, I heard a teaching that we have misinterpreted that verse, but even if that is true, we have witnessed and experienced sins, ungodly beliefs, curses, and diseases that have been passed on to succeeding generations.

Having a sin that has continued generation after generation adds a greater dynamic to its power in our lives. Just as we are born sinners because of being birthed into the Adamic race (after Adam and Eve) and need the redemption that Jesus purchased for us on the cross, our generational lines also need redemption from their sins, curses, and spirits. We are guilty of our ancestors' sins that have been passed on to us because we were birthed into their family and are part of their inheritance—good and bad. The good news for us is that God's requirement for removal of sin and its consequences is repentance.

Imagine two children from different families who are enjoying life, and they each tell a lie. For one it may just be a poor choice; he learns his lesson and decides he doesn't want to lie again. The other child may not think too much about it as he tells his first lie, but for him, it seems to draw him in, and he continues to lie. Somehow, he likes the results he gets and decides it's not such a bad thing to do, and his lifestyle of lying has begun. If they each were standing at the edge of the "Lie River," the child who doesn't have a generational or ancestral history of lying as a lifestyle will find as he steps into the water that for him it's like a small creek that doesn't hold much power, and he's able to step out without much effort. The child who has a family history of lying and deception will find the water like a fast-running river which quickly pulls him in. The stronger the power of the water (the generational sin), the more difficult it is to not actively become involved.

I know the experience of a child who was adopted as an infant. When he was twelve years old, he was part of a sport's celebration party at his friend's house where alcohol was served to everyone, even to minors. He said that when he took that first drink of beer, he was hooked; he actually felt it take hold of him. From that moment on he could taste it, cravingly desired it, and started doing everything in his power to get the next drink, then the next, then the next; and so went his life for decades. It was learned that his birth mother was a severe alcoholic. As a "dry" adult, he knows that one drink would never be only one drink. For him that river still rages, and he knows that if he would choose to "try the waters," he would be instantly engulfed and swept away. Abstinence and self-control are to be commended, but how much more victorious to allow Jesus to remove the spiritual oppression and set us free?

Whenever there is a generational sin, spirit, or curse in a family, Satan will do whatever he can to accomplish it in the lives of each member of the family. For example, if it is addiction, they may each be addicted to something different or have it affect their lives in a different manner, but it is still rooted in some form of addictive behavior or dependence on something other than God. Amazingly, it seems that a generational sin may skip a generation or individual from time to time, but its power is not broken from the family line until repentance is offered to God.

One time I was ministering to a family at the hospital because a young woman was found to be full of cancer. A few days after the diagnosis, she went into a coma. As we sat in the waiting room, the Lord began to open my eyes to see what was going on in the family. The dad had attempted suicide the year before and didn't kill himself, but maimed his body very badly and was in a wheelchair; a brother was a paraplegic because of alcohol and an accident; two sisters had babies born very prematurely, each living with a shunt in their heads. I sensed there was a spirit of destruction over the family. Satan's purpose wasn't to kill each one, but to cause destruction in their lives. I felt the patient was in a coma until the cancer could take her life. After explaining this to another brother and their mother (who knew and believed in the power of the name of Jesus), we went to the chapel, and the mother prayed on behalf of her daughter. Just as a parent has spiritual authority over an underage child, I believed she had spiritual authority to pray on behalf of her incapacitated daughter. I explained that when her daughter was released from that generational spirit of destruction, there was a possibility it would release her to die—Satan no longer having the right to try to cause destruction in her body. We prayed and broke that curse over her life, and it wasn't long before she was released from her body in death.

We all have "things" passed on to us from previous generations, sometimes intentionally and sometimes without a conscious understanding. We "instruct" our children and grandchildren by example, lifestyle, values, judgments, spoken words, etc. Just as we can inherit earthly goods because of a printed will or contract, we inherit sins, spirits, curses, and diseases through a spiritual contract. Romans 8:17 tells us that as God's children we are *"heirs of God and co-heirs with Christ."* We have a spiritual contract with Father God, and as soon as we join His family, we are *"joint heirs"* with everything Jesus is and has. We are also co-heirs in our earthly family blessings and sins—just because we belong, not because of what we do.

People in our lives can have a spiritual hold on us. Sometimes our involvement with a specific person will cause us to carry spiritually what they had. Some cultures purposely pass specific spirits or curses to the next or a future generation, and often to a designated person. I don't know if my experience was one of these examples or not, but I do know that the day my pastor declared that my grandmother's grave was dead (she died about thirty years before), I was released from some spiritual hold.

Demonic spirits have ranks and positions of authority like angels do, some being more powerful than others. One time I was ministering to a woman whose generational line included witchcraft and sexual abuse; she had been a victim, not a willing participant. Spirits can only attach to a person if and when there is an access point—sin, trauma, fear, transfer, etc. In order to deal with the ruling spirit, we needed to remove its generational authority and power. Because of God's giftings, some people are able to "see in the spirit realm" more than others; it's like seeing a picture in your mind's eye; you didn't try to think it, and you know it didn't come from your imagination. The woman was one of those who could see what was going on in the spirit realm inside her. When we prayed and broke the generational hold that that demonic spirit had over her, the woman said she could see the spirit and it was livid, but it couldn't do anything about it. If I had ever doubted the importance and power that generational issues and spirits can have in our lives, it was fully decided for me that day.

**Compromising God's best for us:**

What you believe or desire in your heart can hinder God's best plan for your life. In the months following my husband's cancer diagnosis he believed that God could and would miraculously heal him. We had witnessed people whose cancers had disappeared after prayer, and he believed it would happen for him too. A month or so before Ken died, the Lord gave me a dream. In the dream the spirit of cancer crouched in our front doorway looking for an opportunity to come in. It came in the front door and was eating off our kitchen table. I knew it meant that something in our house was feeding it, giving it the right to be there. (Satan is an opportunist; he needs an access point and will take advantage of any opportunity. 1 Peter 5:8.) While this was happening, the spirit of death was on the front porch, standing back and patiently waiting for its time to enter. One day not too long before my husband became bedridden, as I looked at him sitting in a living room chair, I heard the Lord say, "You don't know what he's thinking." Whatever it was, I believe it changed the outcome of his life. I felt the Lord was revealing to me what was being served on our table—the access point. Ken's thoughts weren't sin, just a compromising choice. I don't believe he desired death as much as desiring to be with the Lord and not returning to work. It was not a coincidence that he died during the night on the date he thought he was to return to work—a job he hated. As much as we desire something to be one way, we need to allow people to make their own choices—and be able to gracefully accept those choices.

A teaching from Dr. Ed Smith of Theophostic Prayer Ministries said that everything that happens to us in life first passes through God's hands. I had difficulty with that concept because I do not believe that God gives us sickness. Then, I recognized that in God's hands is everything that He is: strength, wholeness, healing, provision, and everything that embodies our God. When something comes to us and it first passes through God's hands, I believe His desire would be for it to stop there, having to surrender to all that God is, and not reach us. As God also holds us in His hands, we are there with all that we are and believe: every fear, expectation, and belief about God, life, and ourselves. Our desires, beliefs, and expectations can dictate our future and whether or not something has to pass through God's hands to us. God does not violate our personal will. The Scripture tells us that He is a good God and gives good gifts to His children (Matthew 7:11) and that He wants us to prosper and do well (Jeremiah 29:11). In John 10:10 Jesus is speaking and says, *"'The thief comes only to steal and kill and destroy; I have come that they may have life, and have it to the full.'"* God is all about restoration, not destruction. Why would He purposely give us something that destroys us? While I do understand the concept of trials and testing, I still have difficulty believing that God wants us to be harmed to teach us something. When we do go through difficult times, our character, faith, beliefs, and integrity are tested, and how we survive or stand through those experiences determines whether or not we take a step up on our spiritual ladder.

**Death wish:**

Many people have an old death wish still active in the spirit realm. The decision of wanting to die is a desperate attempt to eliminate their pain in life. What the person felt when the choice to die was made the first time (anger, hopelessness, etc.) will be a trigger point to desire death in the future. I know a very young man who, in the midst of extreme anger at school, stated that he wanted to kill himself. School authorities were notified, and the parental adults in his life were informed. That evening he was presented with a knife and told, "Here, kill yourself." Thankfully, in that moment he turned away. Even two years later, after his original decision to want to die, whenever he became very angry, death was still his go to thought. His anger went far deeper into his past than whatever it was at school that had caused him to tap into that anger and again desire death. During ministry, he was willing to forgive people who had hurt him, and he repented of his anger and wanting to die. I asked Jesus to heal his wounds of rejection, wrongful accusations against him, and abuse (I spoke about specific situations), and to fill those places with His love. Because the young man was willing to ask God to forgive him for the anger and hatred he harbored in his heart against those people and himself, we asked Jesus to release and cleanse him from that anger and hatred. We asked Jesus to cover the connections between anger and desiring death with His blood so there would no longer be that trigger point for him. Then, in the name of Jesus, we closed the spiritual death door. From that point on, the young man has not desired death. Praise God!

Many times as life continues and situations change and improve, dying is no longer a focused wish. We tend to believe that the person has outgrown that part of his life. But the truth is, until there is repentance, the potential and possibility of a premature death is always a close option. The problem with not dealing with that old sinful desire is that your choice of wanting to die is still active in the spirit realm, and Satan will use anything he can to fulfill that wish in your life.

I was teaching a class at church and presented the necessity of repenting of an old death wish and closing that spiritual door. There was a married couple who recognized the need to cancel their old agreements with death. They forgave the people in their lives who caused them pain and helped them believe that life was not worth living. They repented of their sin of not accepting themselves as God's precious creation and for rejecting life. They made a conscious decision to choose life and spoke it out loud. We then asked Jesus to close that door. They each had an inner sense that there was a shift, a change somehow, in the spirit realm. They were grateful the door was closed.

One time I was ministering to a woman, and the Lord had me ask her, "How do you not embrace life?" What a surprised look came on her face. Her way of not embracing life was so subtle that she didn't recognize it as a death wish. Even though she believed she would never really act upon it, she often had the thought as she was driving that she could just pull in front of a truck and it would all be over. She was willing to repent and ask God's forgiveness for not embracing life and for desiring death as an escape. Because it was a family issue for her, we also broke the power of generational suicide. Not embracing life is a gentle form of a death wish, but even in its covertness, it is dangerous. I had a friend who, as a young girl, would walk on the outside of a bridge just to "tempt fate." We discovered that she didn't value her life, and that was one way that she expressed it. Every way that we do not embrace life or its value, we open the door for Satan to work in our lives.

**Rebellion:**

Rebellion from earlier in life will stunt or cripple your spiritual growth and can make it much more difficult for you to make necessary changes. It's easy to think when we have changed our mind and no longer try to rebel that our change in thinking has successfully completed the transformation. Lawlessness doesn't stop just because you turn a corner. As long as your address is still on Rebellion Boulevard, you can't fully move out of the neighborhood. You may stay for a while at another location, but home will always be Rebellion Boulevard. until you officially change it.

Rebellion has powerful legs that will stop you from moving forward. When you believe God is directing you to embrace a new thing or move in a different direction, if you sense the Lord instructing you to do or not do something or give up something you don't want to give up, rebellion's legs will wrap themselves around you like an octopus and hold on with everything they have been empowered to do. However, they only have as much power as you have given them and continue to allow them to have. Old rebellious attitudes and behaviors—which are sin—originally gave them permission to grab hold. Rebellion will continue its hold on your life—many times in very subtle ways—until you repent, break its power in Jesus' name, and make the conscious choice to not continue to rebel.

Old rebellion can be as powerful as current rebellion in our lives. In fact, it can be more deceiving, because many times our old rebellion is forgotten or thought to be inactive. It's easy to think, "God knows my heart; He knows I don't want to rebel anymore." You're right, God does know, but the spirit realm and the consequences of sowing and reaping don't stop because you changed your mind. The only way to stop spiritual reaping is through repentance and cutting off its authority and power.

Imagine being held underwater, knowing you need to get to the dock, swimming with all your might, and never being able to reach it. Every time you angrily thought or said, "You can't make me, I will do what I want or I don't care what you say," you tightened the enemy's hold on you. Every one of those defiant, rebellious declarations is like a spiritual cement block fastened to your foot. It will be very difficult to make God-changes in your life until you break rebellion's spiritual power over you and purposefully submit your will to God.

1 Samuel 15:23 states: *"Rebellion is as the sin of witchcraft, and stubbornness is as iniquity and idolatry"* (KJV). Witchcraft is, in part, imposing your will upon another. As long as you continue to impose your will over God's, you are standing in defiance against Him. If dishonoring our earthly father has severe consequences in our lives, imagine the consequences of dishonoring your Heavenly Father! When you repent and ask God to forgive your sin of rebellion and repent for believing your angry and stubborn will was better than God's, you not only will be able to reach the dock, you will be able to climb the ladder to the top.

Many times our rebellion includes powerful promises made to ourselves. When we are hurt, deeply disappointed, or angry because of some situation in life, we will react in a way that seems like it is the perfect answer to avoid that feeling in the future. A child who is teased and feels shame about his clothing may promise himself that when he has his own money, he will buy the clothes he wants or will only buy what's in style. Our self-made promises are a result of the desperateness we feel. When we make an angry promise to never do something, never allow something, or never let someone do something to us again, we have turned our desire for what is good into a trap. Our angry vows will drive our behavior and influence our choices;

they can cause us to do things that are not in our best interest.

Stubbornness is just rebellion in different clothing. There is a huge difference in taking a firm stance concerning an issue when you know what is right and wrong and the reasons for your stand are righteous (in right standing with God), and in defiantly standing up to someone or something because of pain, anger, fear, shame, guilt, etc. Old stubbornness, rooted and established in anger and rebellion, can cause obstinacy and inflexibility in current life situations, and you don't even realize the spiritual connection.

## Control issues:

Control issues are serious, ungodly, and rooted in fear. Control can be driven by believing that if you are in control, then you know what will happen, and you determine the outcome. Fear of the unknown can be a strong, driving force to feel the need to control. A child who repeatedly experienced pain, not knowing when it would happen again, will be desperate to control life situations. A child (or adult) who has been overpowered and abused will be in fear unless she thinks she is in control and can predict what will happen.

Those who experienced what felt like chaos or lack of control in their family as they were growing up can be driven by the fear, "If I'm not in control, no one will be," or "If I'm not in control, things will be out of control." There are times that a child takes control of a chaotic family situation because no one else does. Once that child successfully takes charge and the confusion and disorder stop, the pattern and need for being in control are set in place. It's easy to fail to make the connection between a childhood experience and adult issues of control—especially in those of us who are "take-charge" kind of people. Taking charge is not the real issue, but the reason or need for it is.

A parent who lives in fear often feels the need to control the lives of her children. The fear can be multifaceted. It can be rooted in personal pain from experiencing abuse, fear of looking like a bad parent, fear or shame, guilt, etc. That parent is often deceived in thinking her overprotection and smothering is just keeping them safe—when in reality, it may be to appease her own feelings and fears. Unfortunately, her fearful efforts to keep them safe and protected are often received with anger and rebellion. When a child rebels in anger against parental control, his desire to be free from control is often taken to the extreme by doing things he knows would not meet the approval of the parent. A child can feel the difference in a parent who protects out of love and one who controls out of fear. Those who had significant rebellion issues while growing up probably struggle with some of those issues with God, and many times do not even realize the connection.

A serious problem we can cause by being a controlling parent is that we are the one in control of their lives. A ship can only have one rudder and one captain at the wheel. As long as we are in control, no one else can be. After having a dream, I was pondering what the Lord was trying to show me. I heard, "Michael (my son) doesn't need the Holy Spirit." God knew THAT would get my attention! Then He said, "He can't have two guiding spirits." I knew immediately what the Lord was telling me. I repented and asked God to forgive me for controlling out of fear. Many times that control will need to be severed in the name of Jesus and the emotional bonds covered in the blood of Jesus so they have no more power.

**Sexual confusion:**
The story is told of a woman who dressed in very neutral styles, dressing neither femininely nor masculinely. During ministry

it was discovered that in the delivery room her mother had said, "I don't want it." Although I don't have proof, I suspect that during the pregnancy the mother probably referred to the baby as "It," and she grew up living the identity she was given. After the Lord ministered healing to her, she developed into a very feminine young woman.

I knew a woman who always dressed more masculine than femininely. During ministry, the Lord showed us a picture of her very proud daddy patting Mommy's tummy and saying, "That's my boy." As she grew and enjoyed being outside doing yard work, he would proudly pat her on the head and tell the neighbors, "That's my boy!" Her dad wasn't trying to create sexual confusion, but it certainly happened. She was born knowing she was expected to be a boy, and the confusion about her sexuality was reinforced by his later statements. And when you consider that she was molested by a male, it is no wonder that she turned away from men and was drawn to women. The talk a baby hears and the beliefs of his parents that he encounters while in the womb begin to set the stage for his life. Many babies are born already confused about who they are and feeling they will never be able to measure up to what is expected of them.

In a family line where one gender is preferred more than the other, the baby can be born wishing he were the opposite sex so he would be acceptable. When a specific gender is strongly desired by the parents, the baby can be born feeling inadequate or wishing he were different.

While visiting a church, the lesson was on homosexuality. It was apparent that the teacher was only presenting the next lesson in the book and didn't have personal knowledge or experience with the subject. At one point the pastor stood up and stated, "That's why you don't let your boys play with dolls or your girls play with cars and trucks." I couldn't believe what I was hearing! When a young woman asked a question about those who say they were born that way, we were told that just isn't possible. I was almost outraged. Because of our womb experience, we can be born believing something about ourselves that really isn't true.

A child who is sexually molested may decide that if she were the opposite sex, it wouldn't be happening to her, or she would be stronger and could defend herself. There are other stronger roots under homosexuality, but these experiences help contribute to sexual confusion in a person's life.

**Sexual abuse and molestation:**
When children are sexually molested, it is never fully over for them (even as an adult) until the defilement and anything else attached to them from the perpetrator is removed. Sin ALWAYS carries some kind of defilement. Demonic spirits that attach or connect to the victim during or because of sexual sin committed against them will remain until their hold or reason for being there is removed. If not removed, the defilement and/or spirits will do what they know to do; they will influence to their best ability, draw to themselves what they like, and gratify their desires in any way that will accomplish what they want.

Years ago I took a young man to my pastor for prayer. As an adolescent he had been molested by his pastor. As we prayed, my pastor "saw" (a picture given to him by the Holy Spirit, sort of seeing it in his mind's eye) a large claw attached to the young man's back. Whatever it was, it was there because of the molestation, and he couldn't be totally free from what happened to him until it was removed. What if that claw was a spirit of homosexuality or sexual perversion? What if it was a spirit of molestation or a draw for other predators?

When children are molested, it is common for them to blame their parents for not protecting them, even when the parents had no idea that it was happening. If the child tried to tell, but couldn't; if the message was not received or believed; if the abuser was not stopped or punished; if proof couldn't be established, or whatever, the child HAS TO HAVE someone to blame. Many times an abused child will blame himself; most often the child will carry guilt (often the perpetrator tells the child it is his fault). Very certainly the child will have anger issues, and almost always will have a deep self-hatred. Often, a parent allows a babysitter to come in, takes the child someplace, or allows the child to go somewhere not knowing that the place or person was not safe, and then the child is hurt. When this happens before the child is old enough to be able to reason out the circumstances, the child often holds the parent responsible. It's always a good idea to lead the abused person, even if he is now an adult, through a prayer of forgiving and releasing his parents. If the survivor does blame his parents and holds them responsible, forgiveness must be offered in prayer, whether or not the parents were guilty in any way. Healing and wholeness cannot come if there is unforgiveness in the heart.

**Hurtful or stressful current situations:**
Current situations in life can be an open door to expose deeper or hidden anger. One time Pastor Paula and I were talking about a current situation in my life and she said, "I don't ever want you to talk to me the way you just talked to that person." As I recalled the phone conversation I had just had, I recognized that while my words seemed appropriate, my underlying tone was very angry. When I expressed to her that I might have a little resentment about the situation, she politely but very honestly said, "Well, yea!"

As we examined the issue, I realized I had been repeatedly saying, "I wish I had done things differently." For the first time, I recognized what I was really feeling and believing by making that statement. In essence I was saying to myself, "I blew it; it's my fault; I did it wrong." I recognized that while I was angry at the person and the situation, I was mostly angry with myself. It was apparent that my anger had more power than it should have had for the current situation, so I knew it was tapping into something or someplace much deeper and older within me. The current anger at myself had been stirring and brewing inside me for a couple months. Often self-anger and self-hatred manifests itself in our physical body, and I was living proof of that!

On my drive home I did some serious repenting and forgiving. Because I recognized my deepest issue was being angry at myself (and self-hatred is a by-product of self-anger), I knew that had to be my focus. I forgave and repented for several early life issues that could have opened the door for me to have self-hatred and anger. Even though I had previously forgiven those issues, this had a different slant—anger at myself. Then, I needed to forgive and repent concerning the current situation. I forgave the other person involved and released her. I had to forgive myself for not doing things differently and release the blame I held against myself. After asking forgiveness for my anger and self-hatred, I acknowledged to the Lord that I couldn't get rid of any of that anger and hatred by myself, but if He was willing to take it, I would gladly let Him. What a relief! What a huge difference it made in my body physically and in my attitude. It would have been a mistake for me to just ask God to help me not be angry; I already was and had been for decades! I needed a clean heart, not just the anger lifted.

**Emotional bonds with people:**

Do you know someone who just can't seem to let go of a relationship? Often those people know they should walk away and begin a new chapter in life, but something in them just can't do that. It is never easy to sever a relationship with a group of people or an individual with whom you have shared good and/ or bad times, have developed strong emotional attachments, or on whom you depend. Living through a tragic life event or sharing wonderful times with someone can create a connection that is strong and many times is lifelong. But not all emotional bonds are healthy or godly. When the attachment is empowered by unmet needs, dependence, fear, deep wounds, or inner vows, it will be very difficult to have the ability to let go of the past and move toward the future.

Whether it is the breakup of a personal relationship, leaving a church, or death of a loved one, our inner wounds and needs are exposed, and it can be very difficult to emotionally and spiritually move on. If we feel God caused our loss or at the very least didn't stop it, we can easily turn our back on Him. Deep disappointment is powerful in our hearts and lives. That is where I landed when my husband died. I was so expecting God to completely heal him that I was almost shocked when it didn't happen. I am so grateful that I had been on a healing journey with the Lord for many years before I lived through Ken's death; many of the vulnerable and hurt places inside my heart were no longer there, and disappointment wasn't able to take control of my heart or emotions.

Our emotional tethers are the resultant fruit of spiritual heart issues. When our hearts still hunger for acceptance, if we are not confident in our own worth as an individual, when our hearts are still bleeding and torn from hurtful events, if we are dependent on someone else to be happy or fulfilled, or when our hope for what we thought was going to be a happy future falls apart, it will be very difficult to emotionally leave that relationship. If your personal identity or well-being is dependent on that person or group, you will sense an even greater loss. When our worth, importance, or who we think we are is in our position in life; if it's in what we do, our successes, what we possess, or who we are with, our emotional life is in jeopardy. Foundational beliefs about yourself that are not rooted in value and acceptance are like a foundation that is porous or cracked and is in need of things or people to fill in those empty places to make it whole or strong. As long as our needs seem to be filled, all is well. When a person is removed from our lives, the crack is again open, and the lack or hurt is exposed. Our pain and loss are intensified by disappointment, anger, or whatever else we feel. Most of us are not able to successfully sustain that pain or loss for very long.

When a person is not able to emotionally detach from a relationship, it's like they are attached to a strong rubber band; they may be able to pull away for a time, but they are always drawn back. Many times a person will leave a church and go to another, but somehow just can't seem to stay away from the previous group. We can be drawn back because of a family or emotional bond, personal attachments, or religious spirits. One time the Lord gave me a dream that showed my husband eating off another person's plate; it was someone he greatly admired and looked up to. The man was an admirable person and had a godly character, but I knew the "eating off his plate" meant that there was a greater attachment than there should be. Those bonds can be severed by asking Jesus to cover the emotional ties to the person (or group) with His precious blood and declaring them broken in the name of Jesus.

Some emotional tethers hold us back while others can drive

our behavior. I knew a woman who had been married for many years, and then through events in life found herself single again; she hoped to remarry. Until she was alone, her "hidden" belief about marriage didn't have a need to reveal itself. When a man came into her life, she felt desperate to be with him; she was consumed with that thought. Her frantic need was putting a "pull" on him in the spirit realm—an emotional draw, and he could feel it. When he gave a romantic rejection, she was devastated. During ministry it was discovered that she had many needs left unmet by important people in her life. She was led through prayers to forgive those who weren't able to meet her needs (even though we know another person cannot meet those needs, if we think they should have or wanted them to, we need to forgive). Jesus was asked to fill all those old, unmet needs. Then, the emotional draw was covered in the blood of Jesus, and its spiritual power broken in Jesus' name. An amazing change took place; the desperation she felt was gone, and the man no longer felt that emotional pull. The relationship was able to continue without that defiling complication. Another person who had that same type of emotional draw from a coworker told me that when a person feels that kind of a pull from another person, it's like, "They want you to do something that isn't going to turn out good."

Later, a deeper need, which was the driving force behind the unmarried woman wanting to remarry, was revealed when she had the thought, "I want to be married, because that means I am wanted." Wanting to remarry wasn't wrong, but her need or reason for it was. As long as she was married, the wounded belief of not being wanted seemed satisfied. Once single again, the need became exposed and active. During ministry it was discovered that when her mother found out she was pregnant, because of a bad marriage situation she did not want to add a baby to the mix—thus, the baby was not wanted. In prayer she forgave her mother, and Jesus was invited into the place of rejection in the womb. Jesus ministered His truth to her pain of not feeling wanted, and that settled the issue for her. Once the pain of that rejection was gone, the desperate need to feel wanted (and her resultant belief about marriage) also disappeared. If she would have only repented and broken the belief that being married meant she was wanted, the root issue (the reason behind the belief) would not have been dealt with, and it would eventually have manifested itself in some other way in her life. She is now content to allow God to do whatever He wants to do in her life—single or married.

**Grandchild rejects Grandma:**
A grandmother told me her personal testimony. When she found out her daughter was going to have a baby, she was fearful because they were told it would put her daughter's life in medical danger. She frequently voiced her opinion about not wanting her to be pregnant. Even though it was done out of love and concern for her daughter (in reality, it was rooted in fear), the baby in the womb knew Grandma wasn't welcoming him. After he was born, he repeatedly rejected any love and attention from Grandma. It was very noticeable that she was the only person he refused to go to. He would stop crying every time Grandma handed him to someone else. When he was about one and one-half years old, Grandma recognized that her response to him while he was in the womb was probably why he was rejecting her. She spoke directly to her grandson and told him she was sorry she had rejected him, asking him to forgive her. She expressed to him how delighted she was that God had put him in their family. His rejection of her stopped immediately, and now they have an amazingly close relationship. Praise God!

## Child's response to rejection:

A young woman delivered her baby very prematurely. The infant weighed less than two pounds, and in her fear that her daughter wouldn't live, she didn't allow herself to bond with the infant. The baby survived, and all seemed to be well. Later, when Mom would try to spoon-feed the young child, her daughter would purposely turn her face away and refuse to eat from her mother's hand. Curiously, she would eat when her dad fed her. She was deliberately rejecting what her mother had to offer. A baby is not capable of reasoning why a parent responds as he/she does; it just senses the rejection and reacts accordingly.

## Mommy's girl and Daddy's girl:

A young couple had one child, and Mommy was pregnant again when they moved to another city. Because Daddy still worked in the previous location, he was gone all week and would join his family on weekends. This arrangement continued for quite some time. When the girls were toddlers, the parents recognized that the older one was a daddy's girl and the younger one was a mommy's girl. They realized something about that was not right, and desired to have a bond with both of their daughters. While the girls were asleep, Daddy went into his younger daughter's room, and out loud so she could hear him (remember a child knows and receives things through her human spirit), he repented and asked her to forgive him for not being there with her in that first year of her life. He asked her forgiveness for anything he thought could have been perceived as rejection. He told her how much he loved her and wanted to be with her. Then, Mom and Dad prayed with the older daughter while she was asleep, letting her know they both loved her very much, and Mommy missed a close relationship with her and desired one. Any barriers to bonding or jealousy were dismantled by the parents' asking their children to forgive them and affirming their immense love for them. There was a profound change in their relationships; both girls were able to embrace both Mommy and Daddy.

**Toddler angry at Mommy:**

I encountered a young mother who felt she had to have Daddy move out of the house. After a couple weeks, their two-and-one-half-year-old son started throwing tantrums and being mean, and it was always directed at Mommy. After her son was asleep, we went into the bedroom, and she asked him to forgive her for making Daddy leave. She told him she was sorry that it hurt him, and asked him not to be angry with her. After repenting for many things, she added, "If Daddy could ask you to forgive him, he would; but because he can't right now, I'm asking you to forgive Daddy and please not be angry with him." We asked Jesus to heal the places inside him where he was hurting and to fill the empty places with Himself. What an amazing and immediate change in his behavior. The next day the anger and tantrums were gone. Praise God!

**Wanting to be in the background:**

Imagine a set of twins born before ultrasounds were commonplace, and no one having any idea that a second baby was in the womb. During delivery, everyone was surprised to have a second "bundle of joy" present herself. Because Mom and Dad didn't know they were having twins, the "hidden" baby was not spoken about or prepared for, wasn't nurtured, and wasn't anticipated with love. All her life she has endeavored to stay behind the scenes.

**Preferring to be by himself:**

The time in the womb is significant for a baby to know he is loved and anticipated with joy. It's a time when he is socialized with the rest of the family as they talk about him and eagerly await his arrival. When a mother doesn't know she is pregnant until well into the pregnancy, the early opportunities for the baby to feel received and loved are missed. Because of not having knowledge of his existence, the baby is ignored and left alone. Many times this child will be most content to be by himself, not interacting with others. For some, the desire to not be sociable is part of their personality, but for others, it could be because that was their early experience in the womb. *The Secret Life of the Unborn Child,* written by Thomas Verny, MD with John Kelly, is a fascinating read as it explains from a medical perspective how womb experiences affect our lives.

**Next child too soon:**

A child who is conceived while the previous sibling is very young and the mother is not pleased about being pregnant again so soon may have questions about why he is here or if he should be here (his existence being wrong—which always produces some form of shame), especially if the parents speak about the pregnancy (baby knows that means him) being an accident or wishing the mother wasn't pregnant. That child may grow up to be withdrawn and may not willingly embrace life. When a mother is angry about being pregnant, the child is often born with an angry edge to his personality which could manifest itself through excessive crying, fussiness, or general discontent. Personally, I've often wondered if a colicky baby may have some of these hidden issues.

## Born by caesarean birth:

This story is very interesting. I was visiting relatives several weeks before the birth of their baby. The date for a caesarean birth was planned, but Daddy had several dreams of early labor and delivery, each dream identical. Not knowing for sure if the dreams were from the Lord, Mommy, Daddy, and I agreed that we should release Baby to be born in God's timing. The pregnancy continued, and Baby was delivered by caesarean section on the scheduled date. After birth, every time Baby would go into a deep sleep, she would have body tremors, but the doctors couldn't find anything medically wrong with her. As I prayed about this, I sensed the Lord telling me that baby was asleep when surgery took place and was startled awake by her extraction during delivery; her tremors were a sort of body memory. I visited again when Baby was four weeks old. As I held her, I looked into her eyes and spoke to the innermost part of her being (her human spirit) and told her I was sorry that after we released her to be born in God's timing, she was born on a date planned by the doctor, and I was sorry she was startled awake as she was being born. I asked Jesus to minister peace to her body and take away the trauma she had experienced. The body tremors greatly decreased.

While I was sharing this story with another young mother, she almost gasped in amazement. Her son was born by caesarean section, and they too were puzzled by the body tremors he had when he went into a deep sleep. She was grateful as she felt God was letting her know the reason for his tremors.

What I learned from these situations is that when a baby is ready to be delivered by caesarean birth, it might be good to wake up the baby and tell him it is time to be born. My mind's eye goes to a picture of an excited daddy who talks to Mommy's tummy during the pregnancy to talk to his baby. That may sound silly, but is very powerful in the baby's life. That recognition of the baby's existence and acceptance by Daddy gives the baby a sense of legitimacy like nothing else can do. When Daddy expresses his love and pleasure to the child, not just about the child, it is invaluable for the baby to know he is wanted and loved. That same principle is what I am speaking about here: Daddy, Mommy, or someone with spiritual authority in the baby's life (preferably a person who already has a speaking relationship with the baby) should speak to the baby and say something like, "Baby, I would like your attention, please. It is time to be born, so I'm telling you to wake up and be ready. We are pleased that the time has come for you to be born, and we are ready to meet you."

## God protected Baby Jesus:

It is interesting that as soon as Mary the mother of Jesus was overshadowed by the Holy Spirit (Luke 1:26–38), she immediately went to stay with her cousin Elizabeth. I believe it was for the protection and nurture of the newly conceived Baby Jesus in those first three formidable months of His life. To be and accomplish everything He was designed to be and do—to fulfill the purpose of His human life—Jesus needed the best womb experience that was possible. Scripture says He was *"made in human likeness"* (Philippians 2:7), and God sent *"his own Son in the likeness of sinful man"* (Romans 8:3). Because He began His human life here on earth, that time in His mother's womb was very important and significant. God sent Mary away from any "town talk" and people who couldn't yet fully understand God's plan; Jesus needed to be joyously received and His human existence celebrated. Elizabeth showered Mary and her Baby with praises and blessings, and Mary rejoiced in God (Luke 1:39–56). I get a feeling or sense from this scripture that the praises and rejoicings were far more than a simple, "Thank You, Father, for this baby." Baby Jesus was enveloped in both natural and divine love. From the moment of conception, He experienced full acceptance and rejoicing over His existence. What a wonderful way to begin a human life.

Chapter Eight

# FEELING MISS . . . FIT WITH GOD AND HIS CHILDREN

This chapter is about relationships—our relationship with Father God and His children, and God's relationship with us. It seems most Christians can easily relate to Jesus Christ as their Savior, but many have a difficult time establishing an intimate relationship with Father God. In the different streams of Christian churches, some emphasize the importance of a close relationship with God, others with Jesus, and still others with the Holy Spirit. None of these are wrong, just incomplete. I've come to understand and experience the need to be able to closely relate to all three for me to be able to fully embrace God in His completeness, serve Him effectively, and walk out the call He has on my life. I have found that most of the hindrances or obstacles that we experience between us and a healthy, whole relationship with God as our unconditional, loving Father are the results of the issues in our hearts.

I am concerned that it is fairly commonplace in the religious community for a person, even while actively serving God, to feel unfit in some way. Some may feel wrong or lacking because of the calling God has placed on their lives—they don't feel like they fit in or aren't understood or accepted. While that is an issue of concern, my focus is on Christians who are trying their best to do what God wants and serve Him effectively, but are still struggling in their Christian walk. How frustrating to live what is supposed to be the most victorious life offered to anyone while feeling as if you don't measure up, that you are not all you can be or are supposed to be, and not knowing why or how to change it. Old childhood feelings that you are a failure or aren't good enough don't stop just because you are serving the King of Kings. My heart really grieves for those who struggle through their Christian experience feeling guilt, shame, or fear that they haven't measured up to God's expectations or requirements and have failed Him in some way. You will find that as the Lord Jesus brings healing and wholeness into your life, you will feel much better about your service to the Lord. I have found that the more healing I receive from childhood wounds, the less offended I am by others, and the less concerned I am about failing God.

**Distancing self from God:**
Many Christians walk with the Lord for years, and then for whatever reasons, they distance themselves from God and His people. When we anticipate a "great move of God" in our lives and it doesn't happen the way we expected, it can be very discouraging, disconcerting, and disappointing. Most of us don't handle change easily, and when the change causes greater difficulty and pain in our lives, we find it even more difficult to rise above the circumstances with faith, acceptance, and understanding. It is difficult to embrace a God we think has caused our pain and struggles or who disappointed us.

When we are very disappointed with an individual, we tend to avoid personal contact. Not only would connecting with them remind us of the pain we feel because of what they did or didn't do, it also stirs up our disappointment, anger, resentment, etc. Most of us don't choose to put ourselves in that position. When it feels like we've been abandoned, especially by God, we will strongly react. A sense of abandonment easily turns into rejection, and always at the person from whom we feel abandoned. Those who had abandonment issues from earlier in life will more likely and more quickly interpret current situations through those feelings.

Sometimes our rejection of God is obvious and "in His face"; for others, it could be very covert, surrounded by seemingly good excuses. A person who turns his face away from God because of disappointment or anger, even if it is not a conscious effort, very likely will stop going to church (that is where God shows up), stop having fellowship with Christians who are in touch with God, and probably will have difficulty reading the Bible and praying. An adult who still has childhood anger or blame at God doesn't usually attend church consistently and probably doesn't even understand why. The adult who carries great disappointment or is angry at God may choose to work or take up some other activity that ties him up during church service times; sometimes, he just can't get up in time to go to church; or he may need a day of rest. When disappointment is accompanied with believing you are abandoned or betrayed by God, that person may not just turn away from God or become apathetic, but may choose to take a path that totally eliminates God. He may turn to another religion that doesn't embrace God or one that doesn't actively pursue a relationship with Him. As a rebellious child of God, he may choose to engage in activities of which he knows God would not approve.

## Feeling distanced from God:

We sense a distance between us and God when we are hounded by guilt. 1 John 1:9 tells us, *"If we confess our sins, he is faithful and just and will forgive us our sins and purify us from all unrighteousness."* Even though God is faithful to forgive, we won't feel forgiven if we haven't forgiven ourselves. Sometimes, we are so disappointed by our own actions that it holds guilt, and possibly shame, in place, and we don't experience the freedom that forgiveness is supposed to give us. When you allow the blood of Jesus to wash over your sin and guilt (specifically asking Him to do it) and you forgive yourself, the guilt will leave. Often, children feel guilty for a choice they felt they had to make; when you carry guilt from early in life, adult guilt will have a much tighter grip on you.

Shame puts up a huge wall between us and God. In ministry circles, shame is often defined as: my existence is wrong. How much more unfit could a person feel than to believe he or his existence is wrong? A child may "act out" to defend those feelings, and an adult often tries doing more things to prove his worth. How do you feel worthy to be in the presence of the Creator of the universe, knowing He created you and He doesn't make mistakes, and yet believing you don't have a right to be here? That is only resolved when the lie you believe about yourself is removed and replaced with God's truth.

How much more distanced from God could a person feel than to believe he has sinned too much to be forgiven, or that his sin is too great for forgiveness? Some believe, that because God doesn't like their sin, He can't love them. Children who were punished or belittled when they had a performance failure, or were made to feel they were a failure when they made a mistake, may not be able to differentiate between the two as an adult. They may have difficulty believing that God can love and accept them in their sin. None of that is the truth. 2 Corinthians 7:10 tells us, *"Godly sorrow brings repentance that leads to salvation and leaves no regret."* The key is "godly" sorrow. There needs to be true repentance, acknowledging that what was done is sin, and that you are sorry that you sinned against God. Being sorry that you got caught or that you can't continue that sin is not godly repentance. God is always faithful to forgive when you are truly repentant. If you don't experience feeling released (forgiven) for your sin, ask God WHY; guaranteed, it will be a matter of your heart and not because He didn't forgive.

**Wanting a distance from God's children:**

Some people don't have an issue with God as much as they don't like His children. Far too many people are offended and seriously hurt in and through church situations. Church people (some would call themselves Christians) can be uncaring, nasty, judgmental, critical, and condemning. We all make mistakes and do things that hurt others, but if you are in a godly relationship with the Lord, you will do what you can to bring a good resolve to the situation—sometimes repenting or asking forgiveness, sometimes offering forgiveness and extending grace to the person, and in all cases, walking in love. It may seem strange that I said a "godly" relationship with the Lord. Those who are driven by their religious connection to God and His rules (that's not a relationship) will usually have an intolerant, harsh attitude about people and sin.

Unfortunately, many offended people leave the church, some turning their hearts away from God because of the behavior of His children. When we don't get the offended issues resolved within us, we take our baggage with us into the next relationship or church—and into everyday life. No matter how well you think the skunks in your baggage are wrapped or concealed, their "fragrance" will be the perfume through which you receive or give acceptance and trust. I met a man who had been criticized and condemned for years by way too many "Christians." I suspect my friend and I are among a very small number of Christians he has met that accept him for who he is—not reject him for what he does. How do we ever think we are going to "win people to the Lord" by slapping them in the face or beating them up?

Some, even though they were very wounded by church leaders, will continue to seek and serve God in another church. Those who continue to press on are Christians who truly have a heart for God. However, even though they may have forgiven the offenders, the fragrance and burden of the rejection can still be heavy on them. Forgiveness is only the first step to healing; they need the Lord Jesus to remove the pain of the offense and anything else that is attached to it. While I was ministering to a woman who had been greatly offended and rejected by her pastor, the Lord showed me that it was added to a long list of disappointments in her life. I asked Jesus to remove disappointment from all the places in her heart where it had landed. I could sense her relief as they lifted off. Currently she was in the midst of a difficult family situation, and instead of being able to stand in the strength of the Lord, the pain she felt attached itself to her list of disappointments, and she couldn't rise above it. My heart breaks for those who only know to ask God in a general way to take away their pain and then continue in life with that gaping wound.

Often we take offense at something that was said or done that may not have been intended to inflict pain, but the old unhealed rejection and hurt in our heart quickly perceives it that way. Whether or not offense was intended, the pain and rejection the person feels is real. When you invite Jesus to go to that place of pain, He does and healing comes.

When I invited my mother to church for healing prayer, her first words were, "They don't rope you in, do they?" Her previous experience in church decades before was being put in a position as teacher of a class of very active boys soon after she got saved. Not even knowing how to relate to boys because of not having had brothers or sons, she felt trapped and inadequate. Instead of being allowed to grow as a new Christian, she was pushed to serve in a place of great responsibility for which she was not prepared or comfortable. Because of her experience, she feared going to another church. A bad church experience keeps many people out of church.

## Landing places:

When I am hanging on to a rope that seems like my lifeline, and it is severed, I will land somewhere. All of us have a landing place, our usual emotional go-to when we are hurt, angry, or disappointed. Our landing place is likely to be a well-worn place we established early in life. Most of us don't want to end up there again, but our spiritual magnets continue their pull. The only way to not continue to end up in the same emotional place, with the same attitude, is to allow the Lord Jesus to minister healing and truth to your wounding where you first established that painful emotional response. When your spiritual "sinkhole" is filled in by Jesus, you may land there from time to time, but you won't plunge into its depths.

Why do some people seem to fall into God's arms, and others end up feeling abandoned? The step we take from the current painful event to our resultant reaction depends on our "stuff" that sits on the steps between the two. Our reactions to things that happen to us in life get filtered through our judgments; bitter root expectations; unmet needs; fears; beliefs about self,

God, or life; disappointments; and painful issues that are still active in our hearts. As long as any of those rocks are sitting on our steps, it will be difficult not to stumble there again and again, let alone fall and land there. Those stumbling blocks are like the dead ends in a maze: you don't want to be stuck there again, but you just can't seem to find a different or better way to go. Jesus is excellent at removing the sinful clutter on our steps, and it's usually done one rock at a time. If we do trip on the stuff on our steps, often the disappointment and pain of the moment needs to pass before we can readjust our focus and get our spiritual priorities back in order. That's okay; we serve a gracious and merciful God who is all about restoration.

Imagine your experiences as an elevator in your "building of life." In the midst of a situation where you are hurt, you should have the choice which floor button to push—how you want to respond or react—your landing place, but the "floors" in your life-building were established and identified earlier in life by your response to life events. You may want to respond to the situation with faith and trust in God, but when you already live in the "I'm Afraid to Trust" suite with closets full of broken promises, abandonment, disappointment, and anger, it will be difficult to not go there again; the right-now hurt identifies with past events, and it is difficult to not respond in the usual manner. You may try to land on the "I Am Good and Acceptable" floor, but the "I'm Not Good Enough/I'll Never Measure Up" suite continues to call you back. Trying to redecorate with "Jesus paint" won't clean out those closets that are filled with rejection, anger, and self-hatred.

For those whose building "lobby" or "ground floor" (womb / early childhood) was filled with love and acceptance, you may end up on a floor where Disappointment lives, but you won't visit there for long. You may go to the Anger floor, but because you don't have a key to that lock, you won't abide there. When your ground floor has meeting rooms for Disappointment, Anger (at self, God, parents, life), Shame, Self-Hatred, Guilt, Bitterness, Rebellion, or Fear where you still dine and fellowship, it isn't likely that your emotional elevator will let you out on floors that are Peace, Joy, Self-Acceptance, or Well-Being. You may not even know those floors exist. The only way to change where you land is to clean out the closets and get rid of the garbage. Trying to put a new name on the floor or door doesn't work, but when the hurts are evicted by Jesus, even if you return there from time to time, you will find it is no longer a dwelling place for you.

Regret always took over every time I was disappointed in myself or did something that turned out to be a disappointment. It didn't matter if I went somewhere, ate at a restaurant and wasn't satisfied (I shouldn't have spent the money; I shouldn't have eaten that), or purchased something, the "I wish I hadn't" regret syndrome always hounded me. I discovered that I had created that place of regret as a toddler after walking into a room and immediately wishing I hadn't. Later, I strongly reaffirmed it as a teen in the midst of a horrific event. Once I knew the root of my regret, I was able to invite Jesus into that place. What a relief to no longer be agonized by regret.

Disappointment is a hard landing place. And for me, that place was huge. It was like jumping into one of those children's play pits that are filled with foam pieces. When you get to the bottom, it is not easy to get out by yourself. The more healing I receive from the Lord, the less power disappointment has in my life. It is natural for us to be disappointed from time to time, but when you cannot lift yourself out of it, there is a root that is giving it power in your life.

In reaction to a hurtful event, if you seem to end up in the same emotional place time after time, if you have a recurring belief or thought you think or express, or if you find yourself reacting the same way each time you are offended, it is very likely that there is a spiritual root that needs spiritual intervention.

**Experiencing the Lord's presence:**

Many Christians only sense the Lord's presence close to them on occasion, or never. Some haven't developed a personal relationship with Him that allows intimacy, and many never get into a spiritual environment where the presence of the Lord is freely welcomed or nurtured. How frustrating it is to know there is more of God to experience, but not know how to get it. Imagine being married to someone you love with all your heart and only being able to wave to them as you pass by each other; that is the relationship far too many Christians have with Father God.

Any heart issue we have that hinders intimacy with others will always hinder our intimacy with God. Someone gave a great definition of intimacy: "into – me – you – see." And for many of us, that is the problem. Shame and guilt will not allow intimacy because they cannot allow you to "see into me"; they will allow a religious experience because they like the "cover-up" of doing God things and feeling better about themselves. They don't like eye-to-eye contact for fear that their worthlessness or shame will be uncovered. They will allow you to go through the motions of worshiping and serving, but it will be difficult to experience a true intimate relationship with God.

God is all about relationship. When He banned Adam and Eve from the Garden of Eden (Genesis 3), I believe what broke His heart the most was that He no longer had close fellowship with them. He loved walking with them in the cool of the evening and enjoying their presence, up close and personal. That's why Jesus died for us: to reconcile us back to the Father. If we feel distanced from Him, we need to search within ourselves or our surroundings to find the reason.

There is a correlation in individual's lives that have turned their hearts away from their earthly father through anger and resentment, and not being able to experience a personal relationship with Father God. Bitterness can grow from intense pain and abandonment. When bitterness at God is established, it is like a tourniquet around the heart—no life flows in, and no life goes out.

Many times we sabotage ourselves from getting anywhere near God's presence or feeling His closeness. When we arrive at church or in our personal time with the Lord with our minds flooded with life's issues; angry at someone; carrying disappointment, a disagreement with someone or something, guilt, shame, or an active sin in our lives, it is like taking our mud-coated vehicle through a car wash with it wrapped in plastic. We can't receive the refreshing presence of the Lord when we are wrapped up in our problems. They are like the plastic covering our vehicle; they are a barrier between us and God. We need to lay those things aside and take off our plastic exterior to be able to experience the presence of the Lord.

Most of us can identify when we have a current issue that is problematic for us, but we don't usually realize that our old anger and vows can hinder us from desiring or pursuing a relationship with God. Children who were forced to go to church and hated it often will decide that when they can choose for themselves, they will not go. As an adult, they may not consciously realize the spiritual hold their self-promise or anger has on them; they only know that they don't have a desire or feel a need to go to church or connect with God. Likely, they are apathetic towards God—for many people, rejecting the church is simultaneous with rejecting God. If you hold anything against

God (blame Him), you will not be able to experience an intimacy with Him until you forgive Him and release that offense from your heart.

Religious spirits may sound like a good thing, but I know from personal experience, that they are not a spiritual asset. Jesus dealt harshly with the religious leaders who were more concerned about following the letter of the law and their outward show to impress others with doing righteous things than about embracing and loving God for who He is (Matthew 15:1–11; Matthew 23:1–7). People who have religious spirits may (and often do) crave intimacy with God, but aren't able to experience it. Their hearts can truly love God and want to serve Him; they can burn with the desire to feel and experience closeness with the Lord and have a hunger to be enveloped in His divine presence, but religious spirits do not allow intimacy. Shame does not allow intimacy. Pride does not allow intimacy. Anger does not allow intimacy. Unforgiveness does not allow intimacy. Self-hatred does not allow intimacy. I clearly remember the day many years ago that I determined I was going to experience the Lord's presence in some tangible way. I didn't know exactly what that meant, but I knew I had to have it. On the specified day, I took my Bible, notebook, food, and beverages to our camper in the backyard; I was prepared to be there all day, if necessary. I still remember my frustration; no matter what I did, said, read, or prayed—nothing! After several hours I finally gave up; feeling defeated, I returned to my normal activities, still wondering what it would be like to really feel like I connected with God. I wonder how many times that is multiplied and played out in desperate Christians' lives.

While I don't intend to do an extensive teaching on religious spirits, I do want to outline some types and behaviors so you are able to recognize them. Religious spirit is like an umbrella title with many different types under it. There are religious spirits of <u>tradition</u> (we've always done it this way; refuse change); <u>exclusivity</u> (we are the only ones selected by God; God's chosen); <u>doctrine</u> (we are the ones who have the correct doctrines; you have to believe this way to be saved; things beyond what we believe are of the devil); <u>legalism</u> (strict adherence to rules; believe appearance is godliness); <u>condemnation</u> (being critical and judgmental rather than having forgiveness and grace); <u>self-righteous</u> (pretense of superiority; pride in how good or right we are; critical of others); <u>formalism or ritualism</u> (only follow an established pattern or prayer; no room for God to show up with His agenda); <u>pride</u> (defensive; self-righteous; spiritual superiority); and probably many more.

Religious spirits are always passed from generation to generation, and you can get them from your involvement in a church or denomination that is governed by them. If you or your family embraces a church that has a critical view of other denominations or has a harsh, judgmental attitude toward sin and sinners, probably at least one religious spirit is active and thriving. All religious spirits are judgmental and prideful, and they always deny their own existence. And they love to argue what they believe—especially doctrine. Religious spirits always stop or hinder spiritual growth. Many times fear is a companion to religious spirits: fear of what will happen if we allow the Holy Spirit to move or fill us; fear of losing control; fear of failure; fear of rejection or what others will think, etc. While I believe there can be room for some tradition and ceremonialism in our church services, when God is not allowed to move as He would choose because of how we want it done or have planned it, we are eliminating the possibility of entering into His presence. Several years ago I purchased a box that looked like a crate. When the button was pushed, it said, "Hello, Hello.

Let me out of here." I believe that is what God says to us when we put Him in our religious box and expect or want Him to do things our way.

**Experiences with Dad flavor our perception of God:**
Interestingly, our experience with our father/dad can play a very influential part in what we believe or expect from God. I knew a woman who perceived God as being distant, separate. She wasn't able to feel like she made a significant connection with Him; she couldn't sense His presence near her. Her concept of heaven was that God will get everyone there who is supposed to be there; He and Jesus will be there too, but they will be in their own place, separate from everyone, untouchable. Her earthly experience was a dad who was faithful to his family and did what he was supposed to do: he worked, supported his family, and came home every night. However, while at home, he was usually in front of the TV or behind a newspaper. Even though he was there in person, he wasn't emotionally connected or available.

The story is told of a woman who would go to church on Sundays and experience a very close connection with God. She didn't have any difficulty feeling and believing that God was right there with her, wanting to meet her every need. Even though she experienced that close intimacy with God on Sundays, Monday through Friday she felt that God was a million miles away, and when she needed Him, He wasn't available. Her earthly experience was a dad who worked out of town all week, but when he came home on weekends, they spent the time together having wonderful fun and fellowship.

In whatever areas you could trust your dad to be loving and faithful, those are areas you probably will be able to connect with God more easily. If your dad was not trustworthy—easily breaking promises, disappointing, or abusing you—it is likely you will have some difficulty fully trusting God. Think about how many millions of people have been abandoned by their birth dad; whether it was the dad's choice or by another, God's original plan of family, relationship, and bonding was broken, and there are resultant wounds and spiritual consequences. Thank God for stepdads, foster and adoptive parents, and grandparents who are loving and nurturing, but no matter how wonderful they are to their children, there are still original wounds of abandonment deep inside. I believe that is why some adopted children have difficulty embracing their new parents and their love. It is no wonder that so many people struggle with feeling abandoned by God.

Children who had harsh, demanding, or angry parents who seemed to make the rules more important than the child's needs often have difficulty believing God is loving and kind. I knew a woman who believed God was just waiting for her to do something wrong so He could beat her again; that was her earthly experience. There can't be relationship with the Father with that much fear.

Our father/dad is supposed to be our protector and spiritual covering. When a dad doesn't live up to those God-given responsibilities, there are negative consequences. And when a dad steps over the boundaries of abuse, he not only destroys part of the child by his actions, he also opens the spiritual door for his child to be prey for other predators. It seems there are spiritual magnets that remain in individuals from the sin that was done to them that spiritually attracts or draws the defilement and sin in other abusers and molesters.

You can understand why our early experiences in life so profoundly shape who we are, how we think and behave, and how we relate to God. Because our earthly father is supposed to be a reflection of God in our lives, it's no wonder that so many people struggle with an intimate relationship with God. Even a faithful dad who does the right things for his family can hinder his child's relationship with Father God because he wasn't able to bond with them emotionally. Unfortunately, when a healthy emotional closeness does not take place, most children believe it is because there is something wrong with them: I'm not good enough, I'm not lovable, or whatever. The really good news is that when you recognize this as a problem in your life, you can forgive your dad (even if he has passed away and if he didn't do it on purpose) and ask Jesus to heal those wounds and fill those empty places in your heart. No matter if we are wounded from neglect, lack of nurture, rejection, or outright abuse, it can all be spiritually redeemed.

**Prayer doesn't work:**

Many years ago I remember going to my pastors with my list of prayer issues and concerns. We talked, counseled, and prayed through issues for two hours, and God did some awesome things that day in my life. When we finished and I glanced at my list, I noticed that not one item I listed had been talked or prayed about. I was instantly furious. I knew my reaction was way out of bounds and that it was my issue, but I didn't know why or how to stop it; all I could do was cry and be very angry. We had planned to go out to lunch, and I certainly wasn't going to miss that opportunity! So, to get through it, I had to sit where I didn't have to look my male pastor in the face. My first two immediate clues were: I was angry about the items on my list not being addressed (what I thought was important and wanted), and I seemed to focus my anger toward a male authority figure.

When I arrived at work and went into the bathroom, I heard

myself say out loud, "I went for prayer and it didn't work!" I immediately stopped in my tracks and said, "Where did THAT come from?!" I knew those words had to have come from my heart, *"For out of the overflow of the heart the mouth speaks"* (Matthew 12:34), but I didn't know why, how they got there, or why they had so much venom. In the midst of anger, most of us will say or do what is hiding in our hearts. Knowing that fruit always produces after its own kind, I knew there had to have been times when I prayed and it didn't turn out as I wanted or expected, and I was very angry about it. Asking God to show me the roots, I began to realize that as a child and adult there were times that I begged God to stop something going on in my life, and when it didn't stop, I was angry. There was another time that I asked God to direct me in making a very important decision, and I followed what I thought He told me to do; then, when the end result wasn't what I had hoped it would be, I blamed Him. I had to forgive God for what I thought He did wrong and release those offenses and blame from my heart. I repented and asked forgiveness for my anger and critical judgment against prayer and broke the power of that judgment's consequences in my life in Jesus' name. Can you imagine where I'd be today if I still believed prayer doesn't work or still had anger about prayer issues! That was definitely a God-designed "setup" for me to deal with that old belief. If I'm going to be setup by anyone, I gladly choose God.

## Forgiving God:

This is a good place to mention that there are times we need to forgive God, not because He does anything wrong, but because we believe He did. Any time you asked God to intervene in a painful or fearful situation and you don't think He did, there is a good possibility that you blame Him in some way.

Christians are often quick to deny they have anger at God—because they know they shouldn't have. But in reality, a child who was repeatedly abused or a person who continued to struggle with painful situations in life and begged God to make it stop and it didn't, will very likely have some anger at God for allowing the pain to continue. Our wounded and immature thinking is, "After all, if God is in control and it doesn't stop, whose fault is it?" Or, "If God really is a God of love, He wouldn't let this happen!" Or, "God must not love me, or He would have done it." Adults who are quick to blame God for things—sickness, death, disasters, etc.—very likely have childhood anger or blame directed toward God. Even if you weren't abused or severely wounded, each time you experienced less than desirable situations, there was a potential for planting ungodly seeds in your heart. It is easy to believe that anger is gone after we get past that hurtful situation and move on in life, especially if we don't feel it stirring anymore; repentance and Jesus are the only sure way that old anger is removed from our hearts. When we forgive God and release Him from whatever it is that we hold against Him, our hearts are freed.

If we want to have a meaningful, intimate, trusting, loving relationship with God and all that He is; if we want to be the best that we can be, serve God in a way that pleases Him, produce good and lasting fruit, and have a pure heart before Him, we need to be serious about our willingness to look inside our hearts. So many Christians will someday stand before the Righteous Judge, saved because they accepted Jesus, but with unclean hearts.

Chapter Nine

# QUESTION WHY?

Many Christians believe it is wrong to question God—that in doing so we doubt His sovereignty. Once again, I believe it is our reason for asking—the motivation and attitude of our heart—that makes it acceptable or not. It seems that children who were angry because they had unresolved questions about issues in their lives are more likely to question God as an adult. When our "Why, God?" question is rooted in blame or anger, it is probably motivated by pain. We don't ever need to question God's motives—I guarantee that He has a pure heart and only responds to us from an unconditional love, whether we understand or accept it or not.

However, that is not the questioning I'm addressing in this chapter. I believe we should always ask the question, "Why?" Not questioning God, but questioning ourselves. Some things we do are not necessarily right or wrong, but our motivation for doing them can take the purity out of what we do, even our service to the Lord. I once heard Joyce Meyer say, "God is not the least bit impressed with what we do unless we have the right heart attitude with it." I remember the night my self-idol fell and pride and a religious spirit lost their hold in my life. I had received a prophetic word from the Lord that said that everything I had done for Him up to that point was worthless. I was devastated; that was a really hard word to receive. While

I was pondering if that really was what God thought and if it was a true word from Him, I had a dream; I woke up verbally defending everything I had done to serve God; I was going through the long list of my accomplishments. I knew right then that the word was correct; my defensive attitude exposed my heart. I immediately began to repent and ask God to forgive me. Pride and a self-idol do not want to lose their place of importance in your life. That was a very difficult night, but I wouldn't exchange that experience for anything; it was probably the first deliverance that began my path to freedom. As painful as it was to finally have my spiritual eyes opened to my own sin, I am so grateful God loved me enough to reveal my heart condition and give me a way to be redeemed.

Many of the things we think we are doing for God are really driven by hidden needs in our own hearts. I love to cook and please people with food, but I discovered that my silent driving factor was to be applauded or appreciated and to be acceptable. When I prepared food for someone, I always apologized for something not being right with it and gave excuses for it not being perfect. I was setting the stage with personal rejection before they could by letting them know it wasn't as good as it should be, and ultimately, neither was I. Somehow, self-rejection seems better than rejection by others.

The situation that finally brought my ungodly motivation to my attention was a church breakfast I had planned and prepared. In the midst of my cooking, someone brought in additional food to be sure we had enough. I was really offended. Instantly, it felt like I wasn't good enough. I knew they weren't trying to hurt me, but it was obvious that it touched a very vulnerable place within me. Proverbs 26:2 says, *"So a curse without cause does not alight"* (NASB). This means when something comes that could offend you (a curse), if you are not already wounded in that area (a cause), you probably won't be offended, because it doesn't have a place to land (alight).

The Lord showed me that when I first began to sing as a teen, underneath my desire to serve and praise God, I really liked and needed the pat on the back I received—the applause. I was so desperate to feel good about myself and look good to others that I welcomed acceptable ways to get that approval. I repented and asked God to forgive me for defiling His gift with my selfish needs, for singing out of my pride (wanting to look good to others) and woundedness, and asked Him to purify that gift within me. I asked Him to heal and fill those places in me that needed approval from others. I gave up singing for many years because I still wasn't sure my motives were pure. Appropriate questions might be: WHY do I NEED to sing (or whatever your service is)? WHY do I need a pat on the back to make me feel better about myself? Another uncovering question might be: How would I feel if I couldn't _____?

I wonder how many times as parents <u>we</u> want our children to behave in public so we look good or that our children are not "looked down upon." Certainly, we want them to be socially acceptable, have proper manners, and be courteous, but we also want to avoid that disdainful look given to the parents of an unruly child and hearing their silent question screaming at us, "What's wrong with the parents?" A few months ago I was in a hotel lobby, and there was a young boy at the breakfast buffet who was very active and inquisitive to the point of bordering on being obnoxious. His mother started to apologize to me about his behavior; I could tell that he was not trying to misbehave or be rebellious. I tried to reassure her that his eagerness and inquisitive nature was how God made him, and that it would be to his benefit some day. None of us want to look "less than" in the sight of others, and when a situation seems to indicate that we are "not good enough" or "haven't done a good job," it stirs up our old inadequate feelings. Needing to please people or needing the approval of others is rooted in woundedness. The more healing you receive from the Lord, especially in the areas of your value and worth, the less you will be concerned about what others think.

Here are some indications that heart issues need to be addressed: There is at least one "WHY" under each of these:

- can't get past an offense or let something go; it keeps nagging at you

- relationship or person you can't let go or get over

- particular issue or person that can instantly "set you off"

- you are a perfectionist; require perfection from others

- feel dirty and can't get clean

- driven to excel; overachiever

- need to have the last word; need to have your opinion heard

- you are an enabler; can't say, "No!"

- need to prove someone else wrong; need to prove you are right

- high energy or intensity in your reactions; feel driven to react

- compelled to defend your position

- overly competitive; have to win

- use guilt or shame as a motivator; use manipulation as a control tool

- need to please people

- feel guilty

- have a resentful attitude

- feel people are out to get you

- don't feel forgiven

- compulsive or obsessive behaviors

- feel shame

- something you "just can't stand!"; strong pet peeves

- feel neglected

- had controlling parents; you were/are a controlling parent

- thin-skinned; easily offended; more offended than seems appropriate

- "aholic" of some kind: workaholic, shopaholic, cleanaholic, etc.

- had angry parents or you were/are an angry parent

- feel abandoned in any way; fear of abandonment

- rebellious

- parents' rules were more important than you

- punished instead of being disciplined; you punished instead of disciplining

- felt belittled by words, actions, etc.

- abused in any way: physically, emotionally, verbally, sexually, mentally

- overly defensive about something or someone

- offended because of what was done to someone else; secondhand offense
- impatient
- critical or judgmental of others or situations
- addictions; can't stop a behavior
- feel you can never measure up or do it right; fear of doing something wrong
- need to escape; feel trapped
- easily overwhelmed
- death wish or suicidal
- offended when you are not applauded or appreciated
- have to be the one in the spotlight
- fear of failure; feel like you are a failure
- were an angry or fearful child
- struggle with depression
- particular subject stirs anger, jealousy, pain, or fear within you
- have an area of life you refuse to look at or talk about
- need to control
- too concerned about what others think about you
- feel your service to God isn't good enough
- fearful
- something you need to give up or walk away from, but can't do it
- something in your life you need to change, but can't

Chapter Ten

# THE SPIRITUAL REALM AND YOUR AUTHORITY

The spirit realm is VERY real and VERY active. We need to learn how to take the spiritual authority given to us by Jesus (Luke 9:1–2; Mark 11:20–24; Matthew 10:1) and use it against the enemy (Ephesians 6:12). Demonic spirits know the power and authority of Jesus' name and His blood, and they know how effective they are when used against them. If dealing with things in the spiritual realm didn't have significance, why would Jesus have done it and then tell us to do the same? Mark 16:17–18 says, *"These signs will accompany those who believe: In my name they will drive out demons . . . they will place their hands on sick people, and they will get well."* Pastor Paula's statement: "If God didn't want me to believe it, He shouldn't have put it in the Book!"

Jesus gave a strong word to His disciples in John 14:12–14: *"I tell you the truth, anyone who has faith in me will do what I have been doing. He will do even greater things than these, because I am going to the Father. And I will do whatever you ask in my name, so that the Son may bring glory to the Father. You may ask me for anything in my name, and I will do it."* This word is not just for a select few, but to all believers in Jesus—and it's not an invitation, but a command. A police officer is given legal power by the local law enforcement to do their work; that badge carries the same power and authority for each one who has been commissioned by that organization. Jesus was given all authority by His Father (Matthew 28:18), and when we join His family, we also carry that authority. An officer would think it foolish to not use the legal rights that go with his position and are part of his responsibility. As believers, we need to know we have spiritual power and authority, and our position in God not only entitles us to it, but commands us to walk in it.

We have a right to speak those same things into being that Jesus did. Romans 4:17b refers to calling *"things that are not as though they were";* in other words, speaking God's will into those things and situations that are not of Him. When we speak with the spiritual authority that Jesus gave to us, things don't happen because we say it; they happen because God backs up His Word; He said He will do it. We are not demanding of God, but of the promises He gave to us. God gave us a promise in Isaiah 55:11, *"So is my word that goes out from my mouth: It will not return to me empty* ["void," KJV], *but will accomplish . . . the purpose for which I sent it."* When I pray for someone, I do it fully believing God is faithful and that He will do what He says He will do. I have to believe that if Jesus instructed me to do it and God said His Word will accomplish it, it will happen. It doesn't matter if I don't see, feel, or sense anything happening at the time—my trust is in a faithful God; I fully believe God will work in the situation in some way. So you may ask, "Why isn't everyone healed?" That is a great question; there are so many things that can hinder or stop healing from taking place, but it is NOT because God is not faithful or because He wants you to be sick or die.

Our lack of understanding about if or how demonic spirits operate does not change their influence or activity. Some in the Christian community believe that Christians can't have demons.

As with other issues in life, once you've dealt with them personally, no one can convince you that it is not true. Research and theology are great, but they can't compare to successful, first-hand, experiential knowledge. I don't believe a Christian can be totally possessed by demons, but I have personally experienced them and have dealt with them in other Christians. In fact, the first cleanup work the Lord did in me was to remove a spirit of pride and a religious spirit, and I have no doubt that I was saved and had been for decades; their removal was necessary for me to be able to grow spiritually.

Many years ago the Lord first opened my understanding of how the spirit realm operates through two books by Frank Peretti: *This Present Darkness* and *Piercing the Darkness*. Even though they are novels, they are a fascinating read and pretty accurate as to their depiction of spiritual warfare—angelic and demonic.

The story in Acts 19:11–16 is very interesting and even funny. God had been doing extraordinary miracles through Paul, and some of the Jews wanted to get in on the action. Seven sons of a Jewish chief priest named Sceva were trying to cast out demonic spirits by invoking the name of Jesus—whom they did NOT know personally. Their efforts were, *"In the name of Jesus, whom Paul preaches . . ."* Verse 15 says, *"One day the evil spirit answered them."* Apparently this had been going on for some time, and the spirit had grown tired of it. Can you imagine the look on the brothers' faces when the demonic spirit said to them, *"Jesus I know, and I know about Paul, but who are you?"* That had to have been the moment they knew they were in trouble! Satan and his demons know exactly what happened as a result of Jesus' death, burial, and resurrection, and they know the power and authority that backs up the finished work of Christ on the cross. Because Jesus was not the Savior and Lord of their lives, the sons of Sceva didn't have any right or authority to send evil spirits away—and the spirits knew it. The man who had the evil spirit jumped on them, overpowering all seven brothers; they were beaten so badly that they ran out of the house naked and bleeding.

Using the authority of Jesus' name is a privilege and is not to be taken lightly. For me, learning to walk, live, and pray in the power of Jesus' name has been a growing process. First, you need to <u>know and understand that Jesus gave us His authority</u>. In fact, He not only gave it to us, He told us to use it. Second, you need to <u>believe you have it</u>. The requirement is to be saved, that Jesus is the Savior, Lord, and Master of your life. Third, as you experience using your spiritual authority, <u>it will grow—just like faith grows</u>. I remember a man telling me that he didn't bother God with the little things in his life; he was waiting until he needed something big; and I continued to observe life not going well for him. I don't believe that is how faith and spiritual experience increase in our lives. We start out trusting God and believing for smaller things, then as our faith increases, we trust God for bigger or more significant issues.

The Lord gave me two experiences early in my spiritual journey which gave me confidence that I could do what He told us to do—use the power of His name against the enemy. The first was a dream in which I physically fought Satan and won. The second took place one night in my sleep as I woke up and saw a dark form (head and shoulders) coming up the last two steps. I was not fearful like when you hear a noise in the middle of the night, but just had a knowing what it was. I knew it was a religious spirit trying to return to my daughter. I rebuked it in Jesus' name and told it to leave and never return. I went back to sleep, and it was several days before I remembered it happening. That gave me the confidence and assurance of knowing and believing that, if the Lord would cause me to do that in my sleep, I had nothing to fear.

# Chapter Eleven

# MINISTRY AND PRAYERS

Is there only one right way to pray through our heart issues? Of course not. Many Christians who know how and are comfortable with praying aren't always sure how to address some specific issues. The prayers I've included in this book are offered to help if you need guidance. While these prayers can be a very useful tool for you, they are not a substitute for asking the Holy Spirit for direction, understanding, and revelation for your individual needs and situations. Adapt the prayers to your needs: change names to pronouns, etc. Most of all, understand that it is not the prayers that heal; it is not the person praying that heals; it is the Lord Jesus doing what He said He came to do—heal the brokenhearted and set the captives free.

**Praying with someone:**

If you are not comfortable praying by yourself, ask someone who has some spiritual maturity to pray with you: someone who has a personal relationship with the Lord, who makes a quality effort to live by God's standards, who is not judgmental or critical, who can be trusted to maintain confidentiality, and preferably one who hears, sees, or senses the direction of the Holy Spirit. I'm not describing a person who is perfect, but someone who truly seeks after God and desires a pure heart.

For myself, when I think my issue may be rooted in a lot of pain or fear, I like to have someone praying with me. That person will probably hear from the Lord differently than I do, will have an objective and unbiased approach (it's not her issue), and may have some spiritual insight I don't have. Eventually, you may feel comfortable dealing with most issues by yourself, but if not, don't be ashamed or afraid to ask for help. There isn't any shame in what you need to deal with, but it is a shame not to deal with it.

I remember ministering to a woman who I suspected was feeling intimidated by me. I reminded her that we were both sinners; we each had a list of our own sins—mine were just in different categories than hers.

**Healing is a process:**
The process of renewing our minds (Romans 12:2) and allowing the Lord Jesus to heal our wounds and release us from the things that have us bound is just that—a process. Philippians 2:12 refers to working out our salvation. Salvation from the kingdom of darkness to the kingdom of light is instantaneous when we accept Jesus as our Savior, but the purifying of our hearts and dealing with our wrong attitudes is like the proverbial onion: removing or dealing with layer after layer, issue after issue. As the Lord brings a sin, wrong belief, or attitude to your attention, recognize that He is giving you the opportunity to forgive, repent, and receive healing. I have a friend whom the Lord gave a spiritual picture of his heart. It was full of heartworms—all tightly intertwined. Even if your heart issues aren't as many or as complex as my friend's, each disappointment, wound, etc., can be a stumbling block or barrier to your spiritual growth. The issues of our heart are reasons why we may not

feel saved and why we continue to have old thoughts or desires, critical or troublesome attitudes, ungodly behaviors, or fears.

## Pray out loud:

When you pray, I suggest you do it out loud. If you are praying with someone, you both need to hear what is being said. Sometimes the one praying needs "coaching" from the other person as to what to pray. One time I was praying with a woman, and as she prayed, she talked around the issue by saying things like, "God, You know that I . . ." or "You know that I don't want to . . ." I let her finish and then said, "Pray after me," and I led her through a prayer of forgiveness and repentance, speaking directly to the issue, not about it.

Leading a person through a prayer, phrase by phrase, can feel intimidating at first. I suggest you write out who and what needs to be forgiven and that which needs to be repented of. Having a list will help you not to forget something that needs to be addressed and help you not to be so concerned about what to say. Also, if they take that paper home with them, they have a reminder of what was done.

Even when I am alone, I pray out loud. There seems to be a different dynamic when I hear myself forgiving and repenting.

## Be specific when you repent:

When repenting (which is confessing your sin to God and asking forgiveness), be specific. Repenting doesn't require telling God why and how you did something. It's natural to want to talk about what you did, but don't. Repentance is the time to acknowledge to God that you know what you did <u>is sin</u> (not just a bad habit or mistake), and that you are sorry that you offended Him.

Individualize your issues; don't group all your sins together or all your life's anger into one group. It is not effective to pray, "God, forgive me for all my anger." You need to be specific which anger you are referring to, because each has its own reason for being there. Each area of anger will give you the opportunity to forgive and release your offender; then, you will need to repent and ask forgiveness for your sinful reaction—anger, hatred, resentment, etc. When hurtful things happen to us it is understandable why we have a sinful response—what was done was NOT right and shouldn't have taken place. But we are hurting ourselves physically and spiritually when we refuse to forgive. We don't forgive someone because he deserves it; we forgive and release the person and the offense because our own heart cannot be free until we do.

Most times, we can repent and ask God's forgiveness in prayer, although there may be times when the Lord requires you to repent and ask someone personally to forgive you for something you both know you did. I have had at least three times in my life that I felt the Lord directing me to a one-on-one repentance; be sure it is God directing you.

**Be specific when you forgive:**
Forgiving someone is not telling them what they did wrong or how they hurt you. Forgiving is releasing the person from their offense against you, no longer holding it against them in your heart. Until you forgive an offense, no matter how grievous or small, God is not able to heal you or turn it around for your good (Romans 8:28).

My experience is that forgiving can be accomplished from two perspectives. It is better if you <u>want</u> to forgive, but if you aren't able, you can <u>choose</u> to forgive out of obedience to God and His Word. Mark 11:25 states, *"And when you stand praying, if you hold anything against anyone, forgive him, so that your*

*Father in heaven may forgive you your sins.*'" Our obedience to God is to forgive; when we forgive, we allow God the ability to forgive our sins.

As with repenting, I believe most times forgiving can be done in prayer. It may not be in your best interest to personally tell the person that you forgive him; he may deny the action, say he doesn't remember it, expose you to more danger, or cause you more emotional pain. Holding unforgiveness is an issue of your heart. A person who insists on confronting the offender under the guise of forgiving probably has an ulterior motive—not forgiveness.

Some people feel they can only forgive in layers; forgiving to whatever extent they are able at the time; then later, they will be able to forgive a little deeper. To me, that is an indication there may be other aspects of the issue that need to be addressed so they are able to fully forgive. A good question might be: What is stopping you, or why do you feel you can't totally forgive right now? Deal with the "stopping" issues before proceeding to forgiveness.

**Childhood roots:**

When you are looking for roots to your beliefs, wounds, vows, etc., and the event happened during childhood, you must deal with it from the child's perspective and experience. An adult can reason out why things did or didn't happen or why parents behaved as they did, but the child could only react out of his/her own hurts. It's the "child part" that needs a touch from the Lord. I ministered to a woman who was so afraid of the dark that she had to sleep with the lights on in the house. To ask God to help her not be afraid may sound like it would have been a good prayer, but it wouldn't have dealt with the root fear—when, where, and why she became fearful—and that is where the intensity of the fear was coming from. We asked the Lord to remind her of that first fearful experience. As a young girl she had been locked in the dark basement as punishment and sat on the top step horrifically afraid of what was in the dark that could hurt her (she was told something was there and that it would get her). When we invited Jesus to minister His truth to her as she felt like she was still sitting on that step, she sensed that He was right beside her on the step with His arm around her, and the fear was gone. Later, she told me that she can now turn off the lights and go to bed in peace. Praise God!

**Praying for children:**

If the child is too young to understand, or if a discussion would cause questions that need not to be asked or answered, pray for the child while he is sleeping. Speak out loud when you pray. Just as he perceived things in the womb, his human spirit will be able to receive from you while he is asleep. If the child is older but still under the parents' authority, the decision will have to be made as to whether to address the issue face-to-face or while he is asleep.

When praying for a child, you may find it useful to make a list of what you plan to say. But even with a list, be sure to ask the Holy Spirit for guidance and to remind you of anything else that you should include. As you are praying and asking the child to forgive you, DO NOT GIVE EXCUSES for what you did. This is not the time to try to justify or explain your behavior. The child's spirit will be able to receive your honesty.

**Asking forgiveness on behalf of another:**

I feel it is appropriate to ask forgiveness on behalf of another person when it is necessary for healing. For example: When someone has been hurt by church leadership or a person in spiritual authority, the wrong needs to be redeemed. Because I am in spiritual leadership, I have told the person that I'm so sorry they were hurt, repented on behalf of leadership, asked him/her to forgive us, and then ask Jesus to heal their wounds. I have also repented on behalf of mothers who weren't able to ask for forgiveness. It does not release the person who did the offending, but it does help the one who was hurt.

When my mother was near death, Pastor Paula felt she was to ask God to absolve my mother's sins. Mother was saved, but there must have been some unresolved issues in her heart or life, and God wanted to forgive them.

I clearly remember the day that Pastor Ron called all the women to come to the front of the church, and on behalf of the men who had abused us, he asked for our forgiveness. That was a transformational moment for me. I remember feeling a cry coming from deep within me and a painful, but grateful, sense that someone knows and acknowledges it. That was my first confirmation of being sexually molested. I had wondered about that possibility for many years, but until feelings, thoughts, behaviors, or memories became known, I only had physical and behavioral symptoms that would suggest it. In the next months and years I was to discover it was true. And, yes, believe it or not, there are ways to hide those memories from conscious thought. Many abused people have been judged or condemned when hidden or repressed memories of abuse begin to surface in their minds. It is common for memories to not begin to surface until a person is in his thirties or older. I was over fifty when my abuse began to be uncovered. When buried memories begin to surface, they can feel as real as when they first happened.

# Chapter Twelve

# PRAYERS FOR SPECIFIC ISSUES

These prayers, when offered with sincere forgiveness and godly repentance (2 Corinthians 7:10) will be very instrumental in your healing journey, because God is faithful to forgive, and Jesus delights in bringing healing to hurting people. Some people and situations will require more extensive ministry to bring wholeness and freedom. Usually, each heart issue will have more than one aspect to it, so you may need to pray concerning each "offshoot" that is connected to the original subject. In all cases, when the issue is generational, break the generational hold too. Each step we take toward wholeness is a step in the right direction. When a well is full of polluted water, it is not likely it will become pure with one application of cleansing. When I have a mountain of issues in my heart, the mountain is removed one rock at a time.

The prayers that are designed to be prayed for children can also be used to minister to adults with those same issues; that is how God can redeem the past for them. Take the principles that are presented in the prayers and adapt them to the adult's situation, praying for their specific needs. While praying, take time to pause in appropriate places, expecting God to minister to the person right then. Some issues will receive God's redemption over time, but others will happen immediately. Most adults are more comfortable praying out loud in front of you when you lead them phrase by phrase.

Feel free to copy or reprint these prayers for easier use.

## Prayer of salvation:

- Father God, I confess that I am a sinner, and without You, I have no hope.

- Jesus, I believe You died on the cross and were the ultimate sacrifice and payment for all my sins.

- God, I believe You raised Jesus from the dead, and that He reigns today as King of Kings and Lord of Lords.

- Father God, I repent for all of my sins and ask You to forgive me and cleanse me from all unrighteousness.

- Jesus, I invite You to live in my heart. I confess that You are my Savior, and I ask You to be the Lord of my life. Help me to see myself clothed in Your righteousness and live a life worthy of Your love.

- Thank You, God, for taking me out of the kingdom of darkness and placing me in the kingdom of light and giving me eternal life.

- Thank You, Father, for making me a child of the King.

## Prayer to invite God to work in your heart:

- Father God, I acknowledge that I have lived my Christian life and served You to the best of my ability, but I understand that I may not have always done it with the right motives or from a pure heart. I don't want to continue to produce ungodly fruit in my life.

- God, I cry out to You like the psalmist did, *"Create in me a clean heart, O God, and renew a steadfast spirit within me"* (Psalm 51:10 NKJV). I acknowledge that, even though my spirit was made new when I accepted Jesus as my Savior, there are places in my heart that still need to be redeemed. I choose to do what Philippians 2:12 tells me—to work out my salvation—so I submit my heart to You for cleansing.

- I ask You to begin to *"remove from [me my] heart of stone and give [me] a heart of flesh"* (Ezekiel 36:26). God, please show me how and where I have hardened my heart and how that permeates my everyday life.

- Matthew 5:8 says, *"Blessed are the pure in heart, for they will see God."* God, I want to be able to fully relate to You as my loving heavenly Father, and I cannot do that as long as I have barriers in my heart between You and me. I want a pure heart so my understanding of You is not tainted or limited; I want to know You better. I ask You to reveal my sin, wrong attitudes, unforgiveness, anger, and judgments so I can repent and get my heart in alignment with You.

- Father God, I ask You to do whatever is needed in my heart and life to allow me to have an intimate relationship with You, my Savior Jesus Christ, and the Holy Spirit.

- I ask You to begin to reveal ungodly motives in my life, to help me recognize when You are bringing an issue to my attention, and to guide me in dealing with it. I don't want to just stop bad behavior; I want to deal with those things in my heart that cause me to produce ungodly fruit in my life.

- Jesus, I receive You as my Healer as well as my Savior. I invite You to do in my heart and life what You said You came to do—to heal my brokenness, cause my blinded eyes to see, set me free from those things that hold me captive, and help me to be able to live the abundant life that You have already prepared for me.

- Thank You, Lord, for Your excellent work in me. Father, I ask that Philippians 1:6 be a reality in my life: *"That He who has begun a good work in [me] will complete it"* (NKJV).

- I declare this is the desire of my heart. In Jesus' name, amen.

**A prayer of blessing:**

To minister to a person's worth—for adults, children, infants, or babies in the womb.

- _____ (person's name), I speak to the deepest part of your being, and I bless you with knowing how much and how deeply God loves you; He loves you unconditionally and accepts you as His wonderful creation. You are not a mistake or a castaway. You were designed and created by Father God out of His light—and you shine with the light of God.

- I bless you with knowing God is always with you and always has been.

- _____ (person's name), I bless you with accepting and experiencing all the love that God has for you. I bless you with the ability to receive the healing of the Lord Jesus Christ, and with the desire and determination to follow the leading of the Holy Spirit.

- I bless you with knowing who you are in God and accomplishing all that God wants and plans for you to be and do.

- I bless you in the name of Jesus of Nazareth, amen.

## When you blame God:

- Father God, I repent and ask You to forgive me for blaming You for _____.

- I confess that I have sinned against You by believing that You did something wrong and holding it against You. God, I forgive You for what I believe You did that was wrong. I acknowledge that You do not make mistakes, but that I don't always understand; please forgive me.

- I choose to release the blame, anger, and accusations I've held in my heart against You. Jesus, I ask You to cleanse me from those sins with Your precious blood.

- Lord, I ask You to purify my heart, heal the wounds under my blame, and remove my disappointment. I ask You to fill the empty places with You.

- Father, I ask You to remove anything else that will be a barrier between You and myself or others.

- Thank You, God for Your forgiveness, cleansing, and freedom.

*Note: Many times a person will have a sense of relief, peace, or calm after a prayer like this one. If there is a sense that nothing changed, there is always a reason. Hidden anger usually stops a release. Ask the Holy Spirit to reveal the hold and then address that issue.*

**Repent of specific sin/behavior:**

- Father God, I confess my sin of _____, and I acknowledge that it was not just a poor choice or bad behavior on my part, but it is sin. I am sorry that I offended You and sinned against You, myself, and others; please forgive me for every way that I am guilty.

- I repent for the pain and trouble I have caused myself and others; please forgive me.

  - If it seems there is an issue driving this sin/behavior:

    › Father, I don't want to just stop _____; I want to go to the root or reason it began so the need for producing this ungodly fruit in my life can be dealt with and stopped.

    › Holy Spirit, I ask You to remind me or show me in some way where this started in my life; when was the first time I felt I wanted or needed to do this? (Pause for a moment to "listen.")

    › Depending on the root or cause, you may need to forgive or repent and invite Jesus into that place in you to minister healing to your pain, fear, etc.

- God, I ask You to wash me clean with the precious blood of Jesus and place the finished work of Christ on the cross between me and my sin. I ask for Your standard of righteousness to rise up within me and be my standard.

- Father, I set my heart to seek You and do Your will.

- Thank You for Your forgiveness and cleansing.

**Forgive self:**

- Father God, I haven't been able to forgive myself for _____. I am so disappointed in my behavior and knowing I have hurt myself and others and sinned against You. I feel guilt, shame, and _____.

- I confess my sin of _____ and ask You to forgive me for every way that I am guilty.

- Jesus, because of Your love for me, I choose to forgive myself, releasing the guilt, judgments, and condemnation against myself, and I choose to allow Your forgiveness to wash over me.

  - If your issue is something you DIDN'T do:

    › God, I ask You to forgive me for not _____ when I thought or knew I should. Forgive me for every way that I failed _____ (name of person), myself, and You.

    › I forgive and release myself from the guilt and condemnation I have put upon myself.

- I confess that the anger and hatred I have at myself are sin; please forgive me. Jesus, I need Your help; I ask You to wash over my anger, self-hatred, disappointment, and _____ with Your precious, cleansing blood and cover my shame and guilt. I receive Your cleansing and freedom.

- Thank You, Lord.

  *Note: Many times a person will have a sense of relief, peace, or calm after a prayer like this one. If there is a sense that nothing changed, there is always a reason. Hidden anger usually stops a release. Ask the Holy Spirit to reveal the hold and then address that issue.*

**Forgive others:**

- Father God, I forgive (or choose to forgive) _____ (name[s]) for _____. I release him/her/them and his/her/their offenses against me; I no longer hold it against him/her/them.

- God, if I have blamed You or anyone else in any way, I choose to release You and them and the offense I hold; forgive me for every way that I have held You or them responsible.

- I acknowledge that my unforgiveness, anger, and _____ (anything else you hold in your heart) are my sinful response to my pain; please forgive me. Jesus, wash over my sin with Your precious blood.

- Jesus, I ask You to minister healing to those places inside me where I was hurt and offended by _____ (name), and nullify wrong words or accusations spoken to me or about me.

- Lord, I need Your cleansing from my unrighteousness and that of my offender.

- Thank You, Lord, for releasing my heart.

**Forgiveness and healing for sexual abuse:**

- Father God, I forgive (or choose to forgive) _____ (name) for abusing me sexually, misusing me, violating me, and for sinning against me; I forgive him/her for not valuing me and for using me for his/her own pleasure.

  - If abuse was by a parent, relative, or caretaker:

    › I forgive _____ for not protecting me and for hurting me instead of taking good care of me like he/she should have.

- If parents are blamed for allowing the abuse or not protecting:

  › I forgive (or choose to forgive) my parents/mother/father for every way I believed they didn't protect me or keep me safe. I release them/him/her and the offenses I hold against them/him/her from my heart; I choose to no longer hold them/him/her responsible.

- I release everything I've held in my heart against _____ (abuser), because I know that if I hold on to my anger, resentment, unforgiveness, and _____ that it will only hurt me; please forgive me for my sinful response.

- I confess anger at myself and every way I've hated myself; forgive me.

- I choose to release all of my anger, resentment, unforgiveness, self-hatred, and _____ to be cleansed by Your blood. Jesus, please wash over and through me with Your precious blood that cleanses and washes away sin.

- I ask You to remove every wrong touch from my body and nullify every word my abuser or others said to me or about me; please remove the labels and names that have been assigned to me. Lord, I ask You to speak peace to the emotional turmoil and pain I feel.

- In the authority of the name of Jesus Christ whom I serve, I sever all connections in my spirit, soul, and body with _____ (name of abuser) as a result of his/her sexual sin against me. Lord, I ask You to cover every one of those connections in the blood of Jesus and restore a sense of dignity, wholeness, and purity in me.

- Jesus, I invite You to reach into the places in my heart that were ripped apart because of these sins against me and pour in Your healing; please hold my heart in Your hands and minister Your love to me.

- Thank You, Lord, for Your healing and cleansing.

  *Note: Many times a person will have a sense of relief, peace, or calm after a prayer like this one. If there is a sense that nothing changed, there is always a reason. Hidden anger usually stops a release. Ask the Holy Spirit to reveal the hold and then address that issue.*

**Forgiveness and healing for physical, emotional, or verbal abuse:**

- Father God, I forgive (or choose to forgive) _____ (name) for abusing me, belittling me, calling me names, making me feel like I wasn't valuable, and for causing me emotional and physical pain. I specifically forgive him/her for _____ .

- I release everything I've held in my heart against _____ (name), because I know that if I hold on to my anger, resentment, unforgiveness, and _____ that I am only hurting myself; please forgive me for my sinful response.

- Please forgive me for my anger at myself and every way I've hated myself.

- I choose to release all of my anger, resentment, self-hatred, and _____ from my heart; Jesus, I ask You to wash over and through me with Your precious blood that cleanses and washes away sin.

- I ask You to remove every wrong touch from my body and nullify every word my abuser or others said to me or about me; please cover the labels and names that have been assigned to me and nullify their power in my life.

- Lord, I ask You to speak peace to the emotional turmoil and pain I feel.

- In the authority of the name of Jesus Christ whom I serve, I sever all connections and emotional bonds in my spirit, soul, and body with _____ (name of abuser) as a result of his/her sin against me.

- Jesus, I ask You to reach into the places in my heart that were ripped apart because of his/her sin against me and pour in Your healing to my brokenness.

- Thank You, Lord, for Your healing and cleansing.

  *Note: Many times a person will have a sense of relief, peace, or calm after a prayer like this one. If there is a sense that nothing changed, there is always a reason. Hidden anger usually stops a release. Ask the Holy Spirit to reveal the hold and then address that issue.*

## Break spiritual ties and cleanse from sexual sin with another person:

For some sexual issues, this prayer may not be thorough enough, but it is a beginning place.

- Father God, I come before You right now confessing my sexual sins. I acknowledge and confess that I have sinned against You, others, and myself by having sexual encounters outside of the marriage covenant. I acknowledge there is nothing casual about sexual interaction with another person, and every sexual encounter unites me to that person spiritually and emotionally. Please forgive me for participating in and willingly engaging in sexual sin with every sexual partner to whom I was not married.

- I repent and ask You to forgive me for the pain and trouble I have caused myself and others.

  - If appropriate: Confess as sin, repent, and ask forgiveness for anything you did beyond the sexual sin; for example: breaking up a marriage, stealing someone's virginity, causing someone else to sin or violating someone else's will, etc.

- Jesus, I ask You to go to the wounded places in me that are a draw to sexual sins and cover them with Your precious blood; cleanse and separate me from other people's sexual sins against me and with me. I ask You to heal and fill the needs within me that cause me to desire and need these sexual encounters.

- I release all of my anger, self-hatred, and _____ that have driven me to these sins to be cleansed by Your blood.

- In the authority of the name of Jesus Christ whom I serve, I sever all connections and bonds in my spirit, soul, and body as a result of sexual intercourse and any other sexual sin or perversion with every one to whom I was not married. I renounce and cut off all emotional connections, bonds, and spiritual draws to my previous sexual partners, in Jesus' name.

- Father, I ask You to purify and cleanse me from all unrighteousness; please remove all defilement, shame, guilt, and anything else that attached to me because of my sin. I ask You to place the blood and cross of Jesus between me and any desires for more sexual sin.

- Holy Spirit, I ask You to renew a sense of purity and holiness within me.

- Father, I thank You for redeeming and cleansing me from my sins.

**Generational sin:**
- Father God, I come to You on behalf of myself and my generations before me. I confess the sin of my ancestors and my own sin of _____.

- I repent on behalf of my ancestors and myself, and ask You to forgive us for every way we welcomed this sin, embraced it, and indulged in it. Forgive us for turning to _____ instead of turning to You.

- Forgive us for opening ourselves up to this sin and its spiritual reaping, and I ask You to cover our original sin and consequent sins with the blood of Jesus.

- I forgive and release my ancestors for this sin and for passing it on to me with its limitations and spiritual consequences.

- I forgive myself for participating in this sin.

- In the authority of the name of Jesus whom I serve, I renounce the generational sin of _____ and break the power of all resulting curses through the redemptive work of Christ on the cross and His shed blood.

- God, I ask You to place the cross and blood of Jesus between the generational sin of _____ and myself. In Jesus' name I cut off the generational influence and spiritual reaping of it in my life and that of my future generations.

- Holy Spirit, I ask You to wash me with the precious blood of Jesus and cleanse me from the defilement of this sin.

- Today I receive God's freedom from the generational sin and resulting curses of _____, in Jesus' name. Amen.

**Rebellion:**
- Father God, I confess my sin of rebellion. I repent and ask You to forgive me for every way that I rebelled against my parents, authorities, life, myself, and You.

- Please forgive me for every time I thought I knew what was best and for forcing my will on others. I acknowledge that Your ways are far better than my ways.

- I repent for my stubbornness and disobedience and ask You to forgive me; forgive me for _____ (name ways you rebelled).

- I forgive _____ (name[s]) for everything he/she did that helped me to feel like I wanted to rebel, and I release him/her and those offenses from my heart.

- God, I know that my rebellion and sins have caused trouble for myself and others; forgive me for hurting others because of my pain and selfishness.

- I forgive myself for my rebellion, stubbornness, and disobedience, and the pain and trouble I have caused.

- I acknowledge that my anger, hatred, resentment, unforgiveness, and _____ are sin and a driving force for my rebellion; please forgive me.

- Jesus, I ask You to heal those places in my heart that caused me to want to rebel, and cover my anger and the sin under my rebellion, stubbornness, and disobedience with Your precious blood.

- Father God, I no longer choose to rebel, and I submit my will to Your will. Please close the door of rebellion in my life.

- Thank You, Father, for Your love and freedom.

**Death wish:**
- Father God, I repent and ask You to forgive me for not valuing my life; please forgive me for every way that I have rejected and hated myself and life.

- I forgive myself for all my failures and believing I am a failure.

- I choose to forgive _____ (names) who have hurt me and caused me to feel that my life wasn't valuable; I release them and their offenses from my heart.

- God, I ask You to forgive me for every way that I blamed You for creating me to be inferior and for putting me in the family that You did. I release my judgments against You from my heart.

- Please forgive me for every way that I tried to escape from life and its hurts, for every way I have not embraced life and have desired to die.

- Forgive me for believing death is better than life and that others would be better off if I were dead.

- Forgive me for every way I contemplated or fantasized about ending my life.

  - If you attempted suicide:

    › Father God, I ask You to forgive me for trying to end my life. Forgive me for not valuing my life or seeing the value of living. I am sorry that I allowed the pain I felt to consume me. Forgive me for choosing death instead of life.

- Jesus, I ask You to come and cover the anger I have at myself and life and my self-hatred with Your precious blood; I acknowledge they are sin, and I don't want them anymore; cleanse me from my sin.

- Jesus, I invite You to go to the places in my heart where I felt rejected, not loved or accepted, and pour in Your healing.

- God, I ask You to place the precious blood of Jesus between me and the emotion of the moment when I first chose to die; I ask that it no longer be a trigger for me to desire death.

- In the name of Jesus Christ whom I serve, I renounce my desire to die; I choose life, not death. Lord, please close the spiritual death door that I opened so that it is no longer available for the enemy to use against me.

- I ask You to deposit Your love deep within me and help me not to reject love when it is offered.

- Thank You, Lord, for Your freedom.

*Note: Many times a person will have a sense of relief, peace or calm, after a prayer like this one. If there is a sense that nothing changed, there is always a reason. Hidden anger usually stops a release. Ask the Holy Spirit to reveal the hold and then address that issue.*

## Child angry at parent:

Most effective when prayed by the offending parent. This prayer works well when the child is asleep.

- _____ (name), I have some very important things to say to you. I love you so much and would appreciate if you would listen to me.

- I acknowledge that you are designed and created by God, and I am so grateful that He put you in our family.

- I am very sorry that I hurt you when I _____ (name offense). I am sorry that you felt unloved, rejected, and not valued.

- Father God, I ask You to forgive me for hurting my precious son/daughter. I am truly sorry that I made _____ (child's name) feel like I don't love or value him/her.

- _____ (child's name), please forgive me for every way that my actions and words hurt you; I am sorry. I love you and don't want anything to hinder us from having a good, healthy relationship. Please accept my love.

- Jesus, I ask You to come and minister healing and truth to _____ (child's name).

- Thank You, Lord Jesus.

**Child feels abandoned:**

This kind of prayer is very effective when prayed by the one who caused the feeling of abandonment, but can be prayed by another caring person. This prayer works well when the child is asleep.

- _____ (child's name), I have some very important things I would like you to know, so I ask you to listen to me.

- I love you very much, and I am so sorry that it feels like I have abandoned you; I never want to do anything to hurt you. Please forgive me for every way that I abandoned you and was not there when you needed me. Forgive me for _____ (anything else you did that could have been perceived as abandonment). I am so sorry that you felt alone and rejected.

- Father God, I ask You to forgive me for every way that I have rejected and abandoned _____ (child's name). Please forgive me for every way that I have failed to help my precious son/daughter to feel valued and loved.

- _____ (child's name), I love you so much, and I am very grateful that God created you and placed you in our family. Our family wouldn't be complete without you. I don't want anything to hinder us from having a healthy, close relationship. Please accept my love.

- Jesus, I ask You to come and heal the hurt that _____ (child's name) feels from being abandoned and rejected, and I ask You to minister Your truth to _____ (child's name).

- Thank You, Jesus.

**Child given up by birth parents, abandoned, or adopted:**
Effective when prayed by adoptive and foster parents; also, step-parents. If the child is old enough to comprehend, you may choose to speak this to him/her, face to face. This prayer works well when the child is asleep.

- _____ (child's name), Mommy and Daddy love you very much. We have some important things to tell you, and we ask you to listen.

- _____ (child's name), we are so grateful that God has placed you in our family. We love you so very much and can't even imagine what life would be like without you. You are a very important part of our family, and we would not be complete without you.

- We are so sorry that you feel rejected and abandoned by your birth mother and father (and foster parents or others, if appropriate).

- Father God, we ask You to fill those hurt and empty places in _____ (child's name) with Your unconditional love and acceptance.

- We ask You to minister to every place inside _____ (child's name) where he/she feels unloved, abandoned, rejected, and not valuable.

- _____ (child's name), we offer you all of our love and acceptance. We believe you are God's gift and blessing to us and our family. Please accept our love.

- In Jesus' name, amen.

**Rebellious/unruly child or any child who was rejected in the womb:**

Most effective when prayed by the person who did the rejecting. This prayer works well when the child is asleep.

- _____ (child's name), Mommy and Daddy have some very important things to say to you. We love you so much and would appreciate if you would listen to us.

- We acknowledge that you were designed and created perfectly by Father God, and we are very thankful that He put you in our family; we would not be complete without you.

- We are so sorry for every way that we have hurt you and caused you to feel rejected, unwanted, not loved, not valuable, or not safe. You are important to us; we love and want you.

- Father God, we ask You to forgive us for rejecting _____ (child's name) when we found out we were pregnant. Please forgive us for believing we didn't want him/her and for not immediately and joyously receiving him/her as Your special gift to us.

  - If abortion was thought of, suggested, considered, or discussed—no matter how briefly:

    › Father God, we ask You to forgive us for even thinking we could stop our precious son/daughter's life. Forgive us for every way that we caused _____ (child's name) to feel unwanted and not safe.

› _____ (child's name), we ask you to forgive us for everything that we thought, felt, said, or did that caused you to feel unloved, unwanted, and not valuable. You do not need to fear; you are safe with us; we want you very much.

› _____ (child's name), we ask you to forgive us for even thinking we would want to live life without you. We love you and are so grateful that God placed you in our family; our family would not be complete without you. You are a gift from God and a blessing to us.

• _____ (name), we accept and receive you with open arms and loving hearts. Please receive our love.

• Jesus, we ask You to minister to the deepest part of _____ (child's name) and remove all guilt, shame, fear, anger, and self-hatred. Please pour Your love into his/her heart and life.

• Thank You, Father, for our precious son/daughter _____ (child's name). We receive him/her as Your blessing to us.

• In Jesus' name, amen.

## Desired or expected baby of opposite gender:

Pray this as early as possible in the child's life—especially if child is still in the womb. Even if you never spoke out loud that you desired the opposite gender, your baby knows.

• _____ (child's name), Mommy and Daddy have some very important things to say to you. We love you so much and would appreciate if you would listen to us.

- _____ (name), we want you to know that we love you and accept you as our son/daughter. We ask you to forgive us for even thinking or believing we wanted a boy/girl instead of you. Forgive us for every time you heard us or anyone else express a desire or expectation for a boy/girl instead of who God created you to be.

- Please forgive us for every way that we made you feel that you couldn't measure up to our expectations or that you were not good enough. We gladly accept you as the person and gender that God designed you to be.

- _____ (child's name), we release you from any and all expectations we had about who you are or will be. We accept you as you are: God's divine design.

- Father God, we thank You for the gift of our son/daughter. We are grateful for who You created him/her to be. Please forgive us for desiring or expecting a child of the opposite gender.

- Jesus, we ask You to remove any confusion in _____ (child's name) about his/her gender and sexuality, and we ask You to establish Your identity and sexuality deep within him/her.

- Father God, once again we thank You for the gift of our son/daughter, and we receive him/her as Your perfect gift to us.

- In Jesus' name, amen.

**Rejected baby/pregnancy – baby still in womb:**

- Baby _____ (child's name if you have one), we ask you to listen to Mommy and Daddy. We have something very important we want you to know.

- We ask you to forgive us for not wanting to be pregnant and rejecting you when we discovered we were pregnant.

- Father God, we ask You to forgive us for not immediately appreciating or receiving Your gift of love to us through this baby.

- _____ (name or Baby), we love you very much. We are grateful to God for creating you, and we receive you with loving hearts and open arms. Please receive our love.

- Jesus, we ask You to pour Your love and acceptance into _____ (Baby or name) and touch every place and every way he/she felt rejected and not wanted. We ask You to restore _____'s (Baby or name) sense of worth and value.

- Baby _____ (child's name), we are excited and eager for the day you will be born and we can hold you in our arms. We joyously anticipate your arrival.

- Father God, we are grateful for this new life You have given to us.

- In Jesus' name, amen.

# Chapter Thirteen

# EFFECTIVE PRAYERS FROM SCRIPTURE

One of the most powerful ways to pray for someone is to pray the Word of God into his life. These prayers are scriptures that are reworded to insert a name or pronoun to direct them to an individual. So many times we pray what WE think a person needs. Why not pray the Word and let the Lord move in their lives? I challenge you to pray one or two of these scriptures daily for yourself or someone else for at least a month and watch to see how God will move in that person's life.

## Colossians 1:9–12 (paraphrased)

Father God, I ask You to fill ___(name)  (me)___ with the knowledge of Your will through all spiritual wisdom and understanding. And I pray that ___(he/she) (I)___ may live a life worthy of the Lord and may please You in every way; I ask that ___(name)  (I)___ may bear fruit in every good work, growing in the knowledge of God, that ___(he/she) (I)___ may be strengthened with all power according to Your glorious might so that ___(he/she) (I)___ may have great endurance and patience, and joyfully give thanks to the Father, who has qualified ___(him/her) (me)___ to share in the inheritance of the saints in the kingdom of light. God, I thank You that You have rescued ___(name) (me)___ from the dominion of darkness and brought ___(him/her) (me)___ into the kingdom of the Son You love, in whom we have redemption, the forgiveness of sins. In Jesus' name, Amen.

## Ephesians 3:16–20 (paraphrased)

Father God, I pray that out of Your glorious riches You may strengthen ___(name) (me)___ with power through Your Spirit in ___(his/her) (my)___ inner being, so that Christ may dwell in ___(name)'s (my)___ heart through faith. And I pray that ___(he/she) (I)___, being rooted and established in love, may have power, together with all the saints, to grasp how wide and long and high and deep is the love of Christ, and to know this love that surpasses knowledge—that ___(name) (I)___ may be filled to the measure of all the fullness of God. Now to Him who is able to do immeasurably more than all we ask or imagine, according to His power that is at work within us, to Him be glory in the church and in Christ Jesus throughout all generations, for ever and ever! Amen.

## Ephesians 1:17–19 (paraphrased)

Father God, I ask You to give ___(name) (me)___ the Spirit of wisdom and revelation, so that ___(he/she) (I)___ may know You better. I pray also that the eyes of ___(name)'s (my)___ heart may be enlightened in order that ___(he/she) (I)___ may know the hope to which You have called ___(him/her) (me)___, the riches of Your glorious inheritance in the saints, and Your incomparably great power for us who believe. In Jesus' name, amen.

## 2 Timothy 2:22–26 (paraphrased)

Father God, I pray that ___(name) (I)___ will flee the evil desires of youth, and pursue righteousness, faith, love and peace, along with those who call on the Lord out of a pure heart. I pray that ___(he/she) (I)___ won't have anything to do with foolish and stupid arguments, because they produce quarrels. I ask that You will grant ___(name) (me)___ repentance leading ___(him/her) (me)___ to a knowledge of the truth, and that ___(he/she) (I)___ will come to ___(his/her) (my)___ senses and escape from the trap of the devil, who has taken ___(him/her) (me)___ captive to do his will. In Jesus' name, amen.

## Psalm 143:8–10 (paraphrased)

Father God, I pray that the morning will bring ___(name) (me)___ word of Your unfailing love, for ___(he/she) (I)___ has/have put ___(his/her) (my)___ trust in You. Show ___(name) (me)___ the way ___(he/she) (I)___ should go, and to You may ___(he/she) (I)___ lift up ___(his/her) (my)___ soul. Rescue ___(name) (me)___ from ___(his/her) (my)___ enemies, O Lord, and may ___(he/she) (I)___ hide ___(himself/herself) (myself)___ in You. Teach ___(name) (me)___ to do Your will, for You are ___(his/her) (my)___ God; may Your good Spirit lead ___(name) (me)___ on level ground. In Jesus' name, amen.

## 1 Peter 2:5 (paraphrased)

Father God, I pray that ___(name) (I)___ will be like a living stone, being built into a spiritual house to be a holy priesthood, offering spiritual sacrifices acceptable to God through Jesus Christ. In Jesus' name, amen.

## Philippians 1:9–11 (paraphrased)

Father God, I pray that ___(name)'s (my)___ love may abound more and more in knowledge and depth of insight, so that ___(he/she) (I)___ may be able to discern what is best and may be pure and blameless until the day of Christ. I pray that ___(name) (I)___ will be filled with the fruit of righteousness that comes through Jesus Christ—to the glory and praise of God. In Jesus' name, amen.

Chapter Fourteen

# MY PRAYER FOR YOU

Father God, I lift up to You each person who has read this book and those who will use these prayers. As forgiveness is given and repentance is offered, I ask You to do a deep healing in each heart, life, and situation. Father, I extend the healing anointing You have put on my life to flow into them. Lord Jesus, I ask You to minister life where there is death. I ask You to minister wholeness where there is brokenness. I ask You to minister peace where there is turmoil.

Father, for those who were rejected in the womb, I ask You to do a miraculous work in them. Jesus, I ask You to go to the deepest place of each one's rejection and show Yourself to them in whatever way they can receive it and know You are there with them. I ask that each one will feel and experience Your presence, acceptance, and healing.

Father, for those who didn't receive unconditional love or nurture as an infant or child, I ask You to wrap Your arms around them; I pray they may feel Your embrace and intense love for them. Father, let them feel Your heartbeat, and as they do, I ask that divine life will flow into them.

Lord, for those who carry guilt and shame, I ask You to apply Your precious blood to each situation. Where guilt or shame was put on them by others, I ask You to lift it off and release them from that burden; cleanse them from that defilement. For those who carry guilt or shame because of something they felt they had to do, I ask You to minister healing to each situation and release them from the guilt and shame.

Father, I pray for faithful Christians who struggle with their self-worth. I ask You to go to the deepest places in them where they feel rejected and not valued; please minister Your truth, worth, and love to each one. I ask You to break through the pain and/or religious teaching that causes them to believe their value is in what they do to serve You or others. Father, they need a spiritual understanding, a revelation from You of who they are, so I ask You to open their spiritual eyes; cause the blinders to come off and spiritual sight to be established.

Father, for those who have turned away from You because of disappointment and feelings of abandonment, I ask You to minister into their deepest needs and wounds; open their spiritual eyes to see that You have not abandoned them. Jesus, I ask You to lift off the disappointment they carry. Father, I ask that they will allow themselves to fellowship with You and embrace You as their faithful, loving God. Holy Spirit, I ask You to begin to gather them back into the Shepherd's flock and fold; establish them in a body of believers that will not only love and nurture them, but will also help them grow and mature spiritually.

Father God, for those who desire a closer walk with You, those who yearn and hunger for Your presence in a greater way, and those who desire Your power and anointing in their lives, I ask You to move deeply in their hearts and lives. I ask that each one receiving this prayer can and will go deeper and beyond their religious experience. Holy Spirit, I ask that You will fill each one with the fullness that was promised to believers. I ask You to do such a powerful work in their lives that they will know, that they know, that they know, that You have moved in and established residency in their hearts. Lord, I ask

You to guide and direct them and continue to shine Your light in their hearts and lives.

Father God, I am grateful that You love us so much that You want us to be all that we can be, as free as we should be, and as whole as You planned for us to be. From Hebrews 12:10 we know that You discipline us for our good that we may share in Your holiness. I pray that each one who has received this prayer will produce a harvest of righteousness and peace in their hearts and lives.

In the name of Jesus Christ, the King of Kings and Lord of Lords, I pray and declare these things to be so. Amen and amen.

# Chapter Fifteen

# I ENCOURAGE YOU . . .

. . . to embrace wholeness. Embrace not just the possibility, not just the probability, but the reality that your emotional roller coaster can be stopped, the cars emptied, tracks dismantled, and the whole structure taken down. Even if you're not severely wounded, any pain you carry or heart sins you embrace will put spiritual limitations around you. Jesus said He came to heal the brokenhearted; let Him do it for you. Jesus said He came to set the captive free; let Him open your inner prison doors so you can walk out into freedom. Becoming whole is a process—one healing at a time. Jesus didn't intend for you to limp through life—He is the better way.

. . . to embrace healing. For many years I believed that Jesus could heal, but I didn't understand how it could happen. I have witnessed many physical healings and have seen miraculous things done by our faithful God. I can't even describe the look on a person's face or the transformation in a life when the emotional pain is gone, or the trauma of a situation is lifted, or an ungodly belief is replaced with the Lord's truth because Jesus ministered into a person's place of pain. There is no God like our God! We serve a magnificent God who loves us more than we could even think or imagine.

The amount or severity of our wounding, heart sins, and spiritual limitations is the extent to which we can know and experience God. We can only "see" and experience God through our own stack of colored cellophane. The only way to fully reach the potential that God has already placed within us or to be able to walk in the call He has on our lives, is to fully yield our hearts to Him. Saying "Yes, Lord" when you believe He has called you is only the first step. In order to have purity in our service to the Lord and know Him for who He really is, we need to allow Him to do a redeeming work in our hearts. Jesus died to save us from eternal death, but our healing was on the cross with Him just as much as were our sins (Psalm 103:1–5; Isaiah 53:4–5; 1 Peter 2:24). Jesus came to heal our broken hearts and set us free; to not allow Him to do that in our lives is to miss out on part of His sacrifice.

I know the difference of living in bondage and walking in freedom, and you can too. I used to feel a little disappointed that I couldn't testify that God lifted me out of the gutter of life and saved me from all of that when I got saved. But now, I do testify that God has done that for me—only my gutters were my inner places of pain, fear, disappointment, and brokenness. I am so grateful for a Jesus who saved me from myself. I pray that you too will experience His healing power in your life.

# RESOURCES AND REFERENCES

To learn how to nurture your human spirit:
*Blessing Your Spirit* by Arthur Burk and Sylvia Gunter
Arthur Burk
2367 W. LaPalma Ave.
Anaheim, CA 92801
*www.theslg.com*

Prayer ministry courses, books, etc.:
Theophostic Prayer Ministries
Dr. Ed M. Smith
P.O. Box 489
Campbellsville, KY 42719
*www.theophostic.com*

To learn about spiritual roots of many diseases:
*A More Excellent Way* by Dr. Henry W. Wright
Be in Health
4178 Crest Highway
Thomaston, GA 30286
*www.beinhealth.com*

Great teachings on our early life wounds and how they affect us:
Elijah House (Christian counseling books, courses, etc.)
Box 3786
Coeur d'Alene, ID 83816
*www.elijahhouse.org*

To order copies of *Boundary Recommendations* by Christine Routh:
Call 1-800-917-BOOK (2665)
Or email: *orders@selahbooks.com*
To contact the author visit: *www.hisexpressimage.com*

Womb experiences from a nonbiblical perspective:
*Secret Life of the Unborn Child*
By Thomas Verny and John Kelly

CPSIA information can be obtained at www.ICGtesting.com
Printed in the USA
BVOW08s2107150614

356393BV00004B/26/P

9 781609 200930